THE ESSENCE OF

PROGRAMMING USING C++

THE ESSENCE OF COMPUTING SERIES

Published titles
The Essence of Program Design
The Essence of Discrete Mathematics
The Essence of Logic

THE ESSENCE OF

PROGRAMMING USING C++

Douglas Bell

An imprint of **Pearson Education**

Harlow, England · London · New York · Reading, Massachusetts · San Francisco · Toronto · Don Mills, Ontario · Sydney
Tokyo · Singapore · Hong Kong · Seoul · Taipei · Cape Town · Madrid · Mexico City · Amsterdam · Munich · Paris · Milan

First published 1997
Pearson Education Limited
Edinburgh Gate
Harlow
Essex CM20 2JE
England

and Associated Companies around the world

Visit us on the World Wide Web at:
http://www.pearsoneduc.com

© Prentice Hall Europe 1997

Typeset in 10/12pt Times
by MHL Typesetting Ltd, Coventry

Transferred to digital print on demand, 2006
Printed and bound by CPI Antony Rowe, Eastbourne

Library of Congress Cataloging-in-Publication Data

Bell, Douglas.
    The essence of programming using C++/Douglas Bell.
        p.   cm. — (The essence of computing)
    Includes bibliographical references and index.
    ISBN 0-13-206186-4 (alk. paper)
  1. Semiconductors.   2. Solid state electronics.   I. Title.
  II. Series.
  TK7871.85.E414   1996
537.6'22–dc20   95-45890
                                                                    CIP

British Library Cataloguing in Publication Data

A catalogue record for this book is available from
the British Library
ISBN 0-13-206186-4

Contents

Foreword

As the consulting editor for the Essence of Computing Series it is my role to encourage the production of well-focused, high-quality textbooks at prices which students can afford. Since most computing courses are modular in structure, we aim to produce books which will cover the essential material for a typical module.

I want to maintain a consistent style for the series so that whenever you pick up an Essence book you know what to expect. For example, each book contains important features such as end-of-chapter summaries and exercises and a glossary of terms, if appropriate. Of course, the quality of the series depends crucially on the skills of its authors and all the books are written by lecturers who have honed their material in the classroom. Each book in the series takes a pragmatic approach and emphasises practical examples and case studies.

Our aim is that each book will become essential reading material for students attending core modules in computing. However, we expect students to want to go beyond the Essence books and so all books contain guidance on further reading and related work.

The Essence of Programming Using C++ is designed for a first course on programming, assuming little previous knowledge of computing. The aim is to teach fundamental concepts of programming which are widely applicable and underpin much of computing teaching. C++ is an object-oriented language widely used in industry and is therefore a pragmatic choice of programming language for teaching. Having mastered the basics of programming in C++, you can move on to more advanced object-oriented programming and many other topics which require programming skills.

Computing is constantly evolving and so the teaching of the subject also has to change. Therefore, the series has to be dynamic, responding to new trends in computing and extending into new areas of interest. We need feedback from our readers to guide us – are we hitting the target? Are there 'hot' topics which we have not covered yet? Feedback is always welcome but most of all I hope you find this book useful!

RAY WELLAND
Department of Computing Science
University of Glasgow
(e-mail: ray@dcs.gla.ac.uk)

Preface

This book is for you

If you have never done any programming before – if you are a complete novice – this book is for you. It is written in a simple, direct style for maximum clarity.

What's included?

This book tells you about the fundamentals of programming:

    variables
    assignment
    input and output
    calculation
    repetition using the `while` statement
    choice using the `if` statement
    functions

and it covers integer numbers, floating point numbers and character data. One-dimensional and two-dimensional arrays are also described. These are all topics that are fundamental, whatever kind of programming you go on to do.

This book also describes good approaches to going about the task of programming.

The language C++

C++ is very widely used in education and in real, professional programming. It has most of the features of modern programming languages. If you learn something of C++, you will be able to converse knowledgeably with programmers and computer professionals all over the world.

C++ is (largely) suitable for use by novices, but regrettably has a few aspects which are strange at first sight.

You will need

To learn programming it is vital to do some practical work. You will need a computer with a C++ development system. There are many such systems around. A typical system is a PC with Borland or Microsoft C++.

Applications

Computers are used in many different applications:

- information processing
- games
- scientific calculations.

This book uses examples from all these application areas. We have also included a few exercises which look at the new and exciting idea of artificial life. The reader can choose to concentrate on those application areas of interest and ignore any of the other areas.

C and C++

C++ is an improved version of the language C. In addition, C++ provides facilities for object-oriented programming. C++ is easier to use in some ways (for example, doing input and output), particularly for the novice. So, given the choice, it's better to start programming by learning C++. Once you know C++ it's easy to learn C. Appendix F explains some of the main differences between the two languages.

Object-oriented Programming (OOP)

It's trendy, fashionable and so you want to do it – it's object-oriented programming. Some people believe that you can start doing object-oriented programming from the start. But we believe that you have to walk before you can run. So we believe that you have to learn virtually everything in this book before you can start doing object-oriented programming in C++.

This book does not tackle object-oriented programming. When you have read it, you will need another book in order to learn about OOP. The annotated bibliography (Appendix A) suggests various good texts on this topic.

What's not included in this book

This book only describes a part of the C++ language. It describes the essentials of the language as listed above. But it does not address any of the object-oriented parts of C++. Also it does not go into all the bits and pieces, bells and whistles of the language. It concentrates firmly on the essentials of the language. Thus the reader is freed from detail and can concentrate on mastering the skills of programming.

Different kinds of programming

There are many different kinds of programming – examples are procedural, logic, functional, spreadsheet, visual, and object-oriented programming. This book is about one very important type of programming – procedural programming – as practised in languages like Ada, Basic, COBOL, C, C++, FORTRAN and Pascal.

Exercises are good for you

If you were to read this book time and time again until you could recite it backwards, you still wouldn't be able to write programs. The practical work of writing programs and program fragments is vital to become fluent and confident at programming.

There are exercises for the reader at the end of each chapter. Please do some of them to enhance your ability to program.

There are also short self-test questions throughout the text, so that you can check you have understood things properly. The answers are at the back of the book.

Pointers

One of the central features of the language C is called pointers. Pointers are hard to understand and lead to peculiar programming errors. Thankfully, C++ makes much less use of pointers, and it is easy to understand a great deal of C++ without understanding the idea of pointers. Thus pointers are an advanced topic. For this reason, we have chosen to confine the treatment of pointers to two specific chapters, one explicitly on pointers and the other on strings (which use pointers).

Be stylish!

This book shows you how to write programs that are stylish and how to go about programming with style.

Program style is important because a stylish program is clear, understandable, will work correctly and can be altered easily. Programming in style is important because it saves time, effort and leads to good programs.

Standard C++

C++ is now virtually a standard language and this book sticks to the standard
language. Also, while there are a number of different C++ compilers around, this
book is about C++ in general and is not linked to any specific product.

Have fun

Programming is creative, engrossing and interesting. Please have fun!

Any comments on this book?

If you want to e-mail the author, use D.H.Bell@shu.ac.uk

Douglas Bell
Sheffield Hallam University

CHAPTER 1

You and the computer

Introduction

To learn how to program in C++ you will need access to a computer with software that allows you to prepare C++ programs. This chapter introduces the important ideas of hardware and software. To prepare and run C++ programs you need to make use of a variety of programs that are supplied with your computer. These are described in outline – because they are different from one computer to another.

The computer – hardware and software

The *hardware* of a computer is the parts you can see and touch. Whatever kind of computer you have, the hardware consists of:

- a visual display unit (VDU) – a screen to display information from the computer
- a keyboard, to enter information into the computer
- a box with the main memory and processor in it
- one or more disks, for the long-term storage of large-scale information
- probably, a mouse to select items on the screen
- access to a printer.

A computer is just a collection of boxes with electronic circuits inside them. In order for a computer to do anything at all, it needs some programs inside it. A collection of programs is called *software*. If you switched on a computer that had no software within it, it would be useless. The software needs to be in the main memory of the computer. So computers are set up so that programs are automatically put into the main memory when they are switched on. The software is copied from a disk. This process is known as *loading* the software – like loading a video into a VCR.

A program is a series of instructions to the computer. We say that the computer *obeys* the instructions or that the computer *executes* the program (as in the military 'execute a command'). We say that the program *runs* on the computer. We talk of *running* a program.

SELF-TEST QUESTION
What is a computer? What is the difference between hardware and software?

1

Once the programs are inside the computer, the computer can start to use them. The programs that are automatically loaded and run when the computer is switched on are collectively called the *operating system.*

The operating system

The operating system is usually supplied by the computer manufacturer along with the hardware, or is bought separately from a software company like Microsoft.

The operating system provides us with useful facilities to:

- enter commands from keyboard or mouse (that is, it provides the user interface to the computer)
- run programs that someone else has already written (stored on the disk).

Your operating system may also provide a wealth of other facilities, including:

- display on the screen the contents of files held on disk
- if you are lucky, send and receive electronic mail.

SELF-TEST QUESTION
What does an operating system do?

The filing system

Your computer has its own disk or it is connected to a disk via a network. Information stored on a computer disk is stored in files, just as information stored in filing cabinets in an office is stored in files. It is a program called the filing system that allows us to do this.

Normally we set up a file to contain a collection of related information, for example:

- a letter to your Mum
- a list of students on a particular course
- a list of friends, with names, addresses and telephone numbers.

Each file has its own name, chosen by the person who created it. It is usual, as you might expect, to choose a name that clearly describes what is in the file.

On most computers, a group of related files are collected together into a directory. So in a directory we might hold all letters sent to the bank. In another directory we might store all the sales figures for one year. In another directory we might hold all our games programs.

You need to know how to use the filing system on your particular computer so that you can:

- create a file with a program in it

- display the program on the screen
- run the program.

Unfortunately this book doesn't explain how to use your operating system – because there are so many of them. You will have to do either one or more of the following:

- ask someone to show you
- read a manual or a book
- experiment.

SELF-TEST QUESTION
What does a filing system do?

The editor

The editor is another important part of the operating system. You might think of an editor as a dominating person with a permanent cigarette in a newspaper office. But an editor in computing is a program that helps us create and change files.

An editor provides facilities to:

- create a new file
- retrieve an existing file
- delete text in a file
- insert text in a file
- change text in a file
- move text around in a file.

Different editors provide these facilities in different ways. Your editor may be built into the software package that assists you in developing C++ programs. Again, this book doesn't explain how to use the editor – because there are so many of them. You will need to become fairly fluent at using your editor, because it is common to have to correct programs frequently.

SELF-TEST QUESTION
What does an editor do?

Preparing a C++ program

By now hopefully you will know how to run a program that someone else has already written – a game perhaps. Now it's time to write your own program in C++.

Sadly no computer can directly understand C++. So we have to make use of several programs that help. The programs are, in order:

1 editor
2 compiler
3 linker
4 loader.

We will now look at each of these to see what they do.

We have already met the editor. It provides facilities to alter the contents of a file. You will have to familiarize yourself with the editor on your computer.

Using the editor, key in a first, small C++ program. Do not worry at this stage about what it means. You will see that the program contains certain unusual characters. You might well have to search for them on your keyboard.

```
#include <iostream.h>
int main (void)
{
    cout << "hello";
}
```

Undoubtedly you will make mistakes when you key in this program. You can use the editor to correct the program. When it looks correct, save the program in a file on the disk. Give the file a suitable name. The first step is complete.

A *compiler* is a program that converts a program written in a language like C++ into machine code – the language that the computer understands. So a compiler is like an automatic translator, able to translate one (computer) language into another.

Find out how to run your C++ compiler and use it to convert your program to machine code. In the jargon, you wish to *compile* your program. While it compiles your program, the compiler checks that it obeys the rules of programming in C++. The compiler issues appropriate error messages. It is rare (even for experienced programmers) to have a program compile correctly first time, so don't be disappointed if you get some error messages.

Now one of the great standing jokes of programming is that error messages from compilers are invariably cryptic and unhelpful. If you are lucky, the compiler will indicate (note: not pinpoint) the position of the errors. Study what you have keyed in and try to see what is wrong. Common errors are:

- semi-colons missing or in the wrong place
- brackets missing
- single quotes ('), rather than double quotes (").

Edit and re-compile. This is when your patience is on test! Repeat until you have eradicated the errors.

The compiler creates a file on the disk. It contains the machine code equivalent of your C++ program. But the program will not yet run because it is incomplete. Every C++ program needs some help from one or more pieces of program that are held in a library. In computer terms, a *library* is a collection of already-written useful pieces of program, kept in a file. Your small sample program needs to make use of a piece of program to display information on the screen. In order to accomplish this, the requisite piece of program has to be *linked* to your program using a program called the *linker*.

The library is a collection of useful parts. Suppose you were going to design a new motor car. You would probably want to design the body shape and the interior layout. But you would probably want to make use of an engine that someone else had designed and built. Similarly, you might well use the wheels that some other manufacturer had produced. So, some elements of the car would be new, and some would be off the shelf. The components off the shelf are like the pieces of program in the C++ library.

Find out how to use the linker and run it. It may be that on your system compilation and linking are performed automatically and invisibly. Nonetheless, one day you will need to know exactly what is going on.

Things can go wrong during linking – and you get cryptic error messages once again. Common errors are:

● the library is missing or not where you expect it to be
● you have mis-spelled something in the C++ program that the compiler was not able to check.

The linker creates a file on the disk. It consists of your program combined with the necessary library programs.

Finally you load the composite program into the memory of the computer and run it. If all goes well, the effect is to display on the screen:

```
hello
```

Again, this final step of loading and running may be invisible on your system.

To sum up, the steps involved in preparing a program for running on the computer are:

1 edit
2 compile
3 link
4 load and run.

Things can go wrong at any stage and part of the programmer's job is to identify and correct the errors. Don't forget: it is rare for everything to work smoothly first time. Be careful, be relaxed.

We have only described the editor, linker, etc., in outline – because they differ from one computer to another. Thank goodness that the language itself, C++, is standardized and the same on different computers.

SELF-TEST QUESTION
List and explain the steps involved in preparing a program to run on a computer.

What is a computer program?

The answer to this question is the subject of this book, and it is probably only when you have developed a few programs yourself that you will have a good understanding of what a program is. For the moment, we will explain the flavour of what a program is by means of a few analogies.

When you wash your hair, read the instructions on the shampoo bottle, which are something like this:

> **wet hair**
> **apply shampoo**
> **rub vigorously**
> **rinse thoroughly**

The essence of these instructions is that they are a sequence. You do the first, then the second and so on. You carry out the instructions, one at a time, in sequence, starting with the first instruction. Exactly the same is true of a computer program.

If you have ever used a recipe to prepare a meal, you may have carried out a sequence of instructions like this:

> **open tin of beans**
> **pour into pan**
> **turn on heat**
> **put bread into toaster**
> **wait until brown**
> **butter toast**
> **pour beans onto toast**

Again, there is a sequence to be carried out – and this is just like a computer program.

There is another feature of computer programs that can be visualized using the recipe. Let us examine one of the above steps in a little more detail, waiting for the bread to toast. It involves a repetition, which we could spell out like this:

> **repeat**
> **read newspaper**
> **check colour of toast**
> **until toast is brown**

Repetition like this is a common feature of a program.

The final aspect of programming is making a decision or a choice. The above recipe might say:

if white bread is wanted
then
   put white bread in the toaster
else
   put brown bread in the toaster

and, again, this sort of decision is a common element of a program.

To sum up, a program consists of instructions to a computer. The instructions involve a combination of:

- sequence
- repetition
- choice.

There are a number of other sets of instructions in common use that have many similarities with computer programs:

- musical scores
- instructions for putting together 'self-assembly' furniture
- knitting patterns.

SELF-TEST QUESTION
What is a computer program?

Programming pitfalls

When you are editing a program, save it every 10 minutes or so to guard against losing your work should the computer fail.

Summary

- Hardware is those things you can see and touch — like the keyboard and screen.
- A computer obeys a program. A program is a series of instructions for a computer.
- Software is the name given to a collection of programs.
- For a computer to work, software has to be loaded into the main memory of the computer.
- The operating system is a collection of useful programs.
- Information held on a disk is held in files. The filing system is the software that organizes files.
- The editor is the program that allows us to change files.
- Compiling a C++ program converts it to machine language.

- Linking a program combines a program with the necessary parts from a library.

Exercises

1 Learn about the facilities available on your computer to:
   run programs
   store information in files
   edit files.
2 Run a program that has already been written – a game perhaps.
3 Using the editor, key in the following C++ program.

```
#include <iostream.h>
int main (void)
{
    cout << "hello";
}
```

Be careful, because it contains lots of unusual characters. When you have keyed it in, check that it is correct, and, if necessary, correct it using the editor.

Then compile, link and run the program. You will probably encounter errors that require you to go back and amend the program. Be patient; everyone makes mistakes at programming.

CHAPTER 2

Data and actions

Introduction

In this chapter we introduce the main concepts of programming:

- data
- input
- output
- sequence.

We shall use the simplest of C++ programs to illustrate these concepts. This lays the foundations for what is to follow.

The simplest program

This is one of the simplest C++ programs that it is possible to write:

```
#include <iostream.h>
int main (void)
{
    cout << "hello";
}
```

It contains several ingredients that we shall not explain for some time. This is because C++ was not designed as a learning language for novices and even the simplest program has some fairly sophisticated ideas present in it. So, for the moment, you will have to ignore some parts of the program. All will be revealed in due time.

Try to ignore everything except the line:

```
cout << "hello";
```

which is the guts of this program. This statement instructs the computer to output the message in double quotes to the VDU screen. When the program runs, we should see the following displayed on the screen:

```
hello
```

which is not absolutely fabulous – but it's a start.

The word cout is short for 'character output'. cout is a function, provided by C++, that performs the output of characters to the screen. The letters in the word hello are characters. The << always follow the cout. One way to understand << is that they are arrows. The characters in quotes are being sent in the direction of the arrows towards the cout function.

We'll now add to the program so that more things are output:

```
#include <iostream.h>
int main (void)
{
    cout << "hello ";
    cout << "How are you?";
}
```

We now have two cout statements. The computer obeys them in turn, one after the other, so that the effect of running this program is:

```
hello How are you?
```

It would be nice to have some new lines in here, which is easy:

```
#include <iostream.h>
int main (void)
{
    cout << "hello";
    cout << endl;
    cout << "How are you?";
}
```

so that now the output is:

```
hello
How are you?
```

When sent to cout, the word endl (short for end of line) instructs the computer to go to a new line on the screen.

We'll finally add a little more to the program:

```
#include <iostream.h>
int main (void)
{
    cout << "hello";
    cout << endl;
```

```
        cout << "How are you?";
        cout << endl;
        cout << "Tell me your name";
}
```

and we are sure that you will know what this does.

A crucial point to recognize is that the computer obeys one C++ statement after another. It executes statements in sequence. This feature is true of all *procedural* programming languages, which include Ada, C, Basic, FORTRAN, COBOL, Modula. If you get the statements in the wrong order, the result could be catastrophic:

```
#include <iostream.h>
int main (void)
{
        cout << "Doug ";
        cout << "owes ";
        cout << "You ";
        cout << "£1000";
}
```

Notice that (almost) every statement ends with a semi-colon. This is one of the general rules of programming in C++.

We can use a shortcut with cout. The above can be re-written like this:

```
#include <iostream.h>
int main (void)
{
        cout << "hello" << endl << "How are you?" << endl;
        cout << "Tell me your name" << endl;
}
```

with the items to be output separated by repeated <<.

We have now looked at two ideas:

- the idea of a program as a sequence of actions
- how to display text on the screen.

Variables

We have already seen that a program consists of a sequence of actions. The next idea is that of a variable. Every program consists of two ingredients:

- a sequence of actions
- the data that is acted upon.

As we shall see, data can be numbers, letters of the alphabet or other, more complex items. Both the actions and the data are held in main memory of the computer when the program is executing. We don't need to worry about *where* in the memory they are – that's the beauty of programming in a language like C++.

Data in a program is held in things called variables. A variable is a place in main memory that holds a piece of data. A variable has a name, given to it by the programmer. For the time being, we are going to look at data that is simple numbers. So the declaration:

```
int alice;
```

tells the C++ compiler to set up a place in memory to hold an integer number. The place is called alice.

It may help to picture a variable as a box in memory:

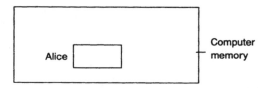

A variable like this has no useful value in it (for now). We can place a value in a variable by instructing the computer to input a value from the keyboard and to put the value in the variable. The C++ looks like this:

```
int alice;
cin >> alice;
```

cin (short for character input) directs the computer to wait until the human has keyed in a number on the keyboard. It then places the value in the variable that is named. Suppose then that we run the program and that the human keys in the value 29. Then after the input, the variable will have in it the value 29:

Alice [29]

We could next instruct the computer to simply display the value contained in alice on the screen:

```
cout << alice;
```

cout is short for character output. Notice that the arrows, <<, point to the left.

So here now is a complete C++ program to input an integer number and to echo it back to the screen:

```
#include <iostream.h>
int main (void)
{
     int alice;

     cin >> alice;
     cout << "here is the echo ";
     cout << alice;
}
```

SELF-TEST QUESTION
What is wrong with this?

```
cin << alice;
```

We will complete the story on what `cin` does. If a program says:

```
int number;
cin >> number;
```

then the computer looks for some input from the computer keyboard. If any spaces are entered, they are ignored. So are newlines and tabs. When some digits are entered, they are regarded as being the number, an integer. The end of the number is taken to be anything other than a digit – a space, newline, tab or any other non-digit character. So suitable input to the program fragment above would be any of the following:

```
456 newline
34space
678,
```

Names

Every variable has its own name. The variable used above was called alice. Choosing suitable names is just one of the many areas where the programmer has scope for creativity.

There's plenty of scope for imagination because:

- names can consist of letters, digits and underlines
- names can be as long as you like

provided that:

- a name starts with a letter
- a name is unique (different from any other name in the program) somewhere in its first 32 characters.

Typical examples of variable names are:

count, Sum, salary, next_character, total, reply, Net_Pay

The usual advice on choosing names is to make them as meaningful as possible. This is to help make programs clear and understandable.

Be careful, because the names Doug and doug are different. The difference between upper and lower case does matter. If you write:

```
int Doug;
cin >> doug;
```

you will get a compilation error.

SELF-TEST QUESTION
Which of these potential names are valid and which are invalid. Why?

running_total, main, 1st_value, SUM, again, Salary_for_1999, cost-code

Assignment

We have seen that one way of giving a variable a value is to input a number from the keyboard. Another important way is to use an assignment statement. Look at this program fragment:

```
int alice, bill;

cin >> alice;
bill = alice;
cout << bill;
```

Two integer variables called alice and bill are declared. Then a value for alice (an integer) is input from the keyboard.

Next is the assignment statement. Forget whatever you already know about what = means. In programming = means 'becomes equal to' or simply 'becomes'. So, the statement reads 'bill becomes equal to the value of alice'. Put another way, the value in alice is copied into the variable bill.

Finally the value of the variable bill is displayed on the screen.

Assignments are frequently used in programming. They are used whenever the program changes the value of a variable.

Carefully check what the following program extract achieves:

```
int Alice, Tom;

cin >> Alice >> Tom;

Alice = Tom;
Tom = Alice;

cout << Alice << Tom;
```

Superficially it may look as if the program interchanges the two values. Make sure that you understand that it does not.

Now look at the following piece of program and convince yourself that it successfully interchanges the values:

```
int Alice, Tom, Save;

cin >> Alice >> Tom;

Save = Alice;
Alice = Tom;
Tom = Save;

cout << Alice << Tom;
```

Simple calculations

Assignments are also used to carry out simple arithmetic. For example, suppose we want a program to input two numbers and then add them together:

```
int mine, yours, sum;

cin >> mine >> yours;
sum = mine+yours;
cout << sum;
```

This time the value of the variable sum becomes equal to the value of mine plus the value of yours. If we run this program and enter two numbers:

23   69

the program will output their sum:

    92

So we now have a little piece of program to do addition.

We can make this program more user-friendly if we make it carry out a dialogue with the user like this:

Please enter two numbers

23   69

The sum is 92

The complete program to do this is:

```
#include <iostream.h>
int main (void)
{
int a, b, sum;

cout << "Please enter two numbers" << endl;
cin >> a >> b;
sum = a+b;
cout << "The sum is ";
cout << sum;
}
```

We have seen how to do addition. Subtraction is very similar:

```
int a, b, difference;

cin >> a >> b;
difference = a - b;
```

There is one particular calculation that is used extremely often. It is the calculation to add one to the value of an integer. If the integer variable is called x, we can add the value one like this:

```
x = x+1;
```

Some novices to programming find this statement a little strange – because the variable (x) appears twice. The way to interpret this statement is to read the right hand side first. The right hand side says 'Take the value of x and add the number one to it'. Now carry out the remainder of the statement, which is 'Give the value to the variable x'.

In the jargon of programming, adding one to the value of a variable is sometimes called *incrementing* the value.

This calculation is used so often that it has a shorthand:

```
x++;   means   x = x+1;  or 'add one to x'
```

We have seen how to carry out simple calculations. More complex calculations are explained in Chapter 5.

SELF-TEST QUESTIONS

What does this piece of program do?

```
int year_of_birth, year_is_21;

cin >> year_of_birth;
year_is_21 = year_of_birth + 21;
cout << year_is_21;
```

What does this piece of program do?

```
int wage, tax, pay;

cin >> wage >> tax;
pay = wage - tax;
cout << pay;
```

A typical series of actions for a computer program to carry out is:

1 input some numbers
2 perform a calculation
3 display the answer.

Character data

We have already seen how text (a series of characters) can be displayed on the screen like this:

```
cout << "have a good day";
```

We can also write statements to process individual characters – declare them, input them, output them.

First, to declare a variable that is capable of holding a single character:

```
char c;
```

asks the computer system to create a place in memory with the name c. We can now input a single character from the keyboard and place it in this variable:

```
cin >> c;
```

In response to this instruction, the computer waits until a single character is entered from the keyboard and places the value in the variable c. The character can be anything that appears on the keyboard – letters, punctuation marks, exotic characters like &, *, @, etc.

We can output a single character, like this:

```
cout << c;
```

so that a simple program that inputs two characters and outputs them in reverse order is:

```
char c1, c2;

cin >> c1, c2;
cout << c2, c1;
```

Just as with integer variables, we can use assignment:

```
cin >> c1;
c2 = c1;
cout << c2;
```

which copies a value from one variable to another. In this case the value of c2 becomes equal to the value of c1.

You can perform calculations on characters, like this:

```
char c1, c2;

c1 = c2 + 23;
```

although this really is meaningless. If you don't believe this, think about adding the character $ to the character *. C++ provides this facility to carry out arithmetic on characters for special-purpose programming. Most programmers would rarely use it, and novices never.

Finally, we can assign a value to a character variable like this:

```
char c;

c = '*';
```

in which we place an asterisk character in the variable c. (Note that the character is enclosed in single quotes, not double quotes.)

SELF-TEST QUESTION
What does this sequence do?

```
char this_one, that_one;

cin >> this_one;
that_one=this_one;
cout << that_one;
this_one = '?';
cout << this_one;
```

Comments

Programmers write comments in their programs to remind themselves (and others) of what the program means. In C++, anything on a line after the pair of characters // is a comment. So, for example, we can write:

```
// increment the count of sheep
sheep++;
```

or:

```
sheep++; // increment the count of sheep
```

Comments are ignored by the compiler and have no meaning except to the human reader. There are different views about how many comments are necessary in programs. Chapter 20 on program style discusses this issue. In this book, we use comments judiciously. We don't use a comment when the program is clear anyway. But we do use a comment when something needs to be explained.

SELF-TEST QUESTION
What is the effect of this statement?

```
// cout << "Don't forget to save your file";
```

Programming pitfalls

Check that you have used >> or << correctly in conjunction with cin and cout. Here are correct examples to emulate:

```
cin >> number;
cout << number;
```

New language elements

```
int
cin
cout
=
char
+
-
```

Summary

- A program carries out a sequence of actions.
- A variable is a place in the computer's main memory that holds a data item.
- A variable has a name given to it by the programmer.
- An integer variable holds an integer number; a character variable holds a single character.
- cin is used to input a number or a character from the keyboard and place it in the designated variable.
- cout is used to output the value of an integer variable or a character variable to the screen.

Exercises

Numbers

1   Key in and run some of the simple C++ programs given above that carry out input, output and simple calculations.
2   Write a program to input three numbers and display them in the opposite order to which they were entered. For example, if the user keys in:

1   2   3

the program should output:

3 2 1

3 Write a program to input a number and output double its value (the number added to itself).
4 Enhance the above program so that it prompts the user for input and also outputs text along with the number, like this:

give me a number please
7
thankyou.
the value of 7 doubled is
14

Characters

1 Write a program to input a single character from the keyboard and echo it back to the screen.
2 Write a program to input two characters and output them in reverse order.

CHAPTER 3
Decisions – if

Introduction

We all make decisions in daily life. We wear a coat if it is raining. We buy a CD if
we have enough money. Decisions are also central to computer programs. The
computer tests a value and, according to the result, takes one course of action or
another.

We have seen that a computer program is a series of instructions to a computer.
The computer obeys the instructions one after another in sequence. Often we want
the computer to carry out a test on some data and then take one of a choice of
actions depending on the result of the test. This is sometimes called selection. It
uses a statement (or instruction) called the if statement, the central subject of this
chapter.

The if statement

As an example, let us consider a program that inputs someone's age and decides
from the age what the person is allowed to do – vote, get married, drive a car.
Taking just the voting age, here is the essence of the program:

```
int age;

cin >> age;
if (age >17) cout << "you can vote";
cout << "good-bye";
```

The if statement tests the value of the variable age. If the value is greater than 17,
the statement alongside the if is carried out. Then the next statement is executed.
On the other hand, if the age is not greater than 17, the associated statement is
ignored and the next statement is executed.

There are two parts to the if statement:

- the condition being tested
- the statement(s) to be executed if the condition is true.

All programs have a sequence of actions. A sequence is still evident here:

1 An age is input.
2 Then a test is done.
3 If appropriate, a message is output to say that the person can vote.
4 Finally the statement to output the 'good-bye' message is (always) executed.

Very often we want not just one, but a complete sequence of actions carried out if the result of the test is true:

```
cin >> age;
if (age >17)
    {
    cout << "congratulations!";
    cout << "you can vote";
    cout << endl;
    }
cout << "good-bye";
```

The sequence of statements to be carried out if the test is true is enclosed in curly brackets. Each statement is followed by a semi-colon. It is also good practice to 'indent' the text that is part of the if statement. (Indentation means using spaces to push the text over to the right.) This is not a mandatory part of the C++ language, but a way of making the meaning of the program clearer to us humans.

The rule is: when just one statement is to be done as part of the if, it need not be enclosed in curly brackets. (But it can be if you like.)

SELF-TEST QUESTION
Do these two pieces of C++ coding achieve the same end or not?

```
if (age >18) cout << "you can vote";

if (age < 18) cout << "you cannot vote";
```

Very often in a program we want to specify *two* sequences of actions – those that are carried out if the condition is true and those that are carried out if the condition is false:

```
cin >> age;
if (age >17)
    {
    cout << "congratulations!";
    cout << "you can vote";
    }
else
    {
```

```
        cout << "sorry";
        cout << "you cannot vote";
        }
    cout << endl;
    cout << "good-bye";
```

There are three parts to this if statement:

- the condition being tested
- the statement(s) to be executed if the condition is true
- the statement(s) to be executed if the condition is false.

The new element here is the word else, which introduces the second part of the if statement. Notice how the indentation helps considerably in emphasizing the intention of the program. Also, each statement is followed by a semi-colon.

Comparison operators

The program fragments above used only one of several comparison operators, greater than (>). Here is a complete table of the comparison operators:

>	means greater than
<	means less than
==	means equals
!=	means not equal to
<=	means less than or equal to
>=	means greater than or equal to

The odd one out in this list is the test for equality, which is two equals signs, rather than one. It is a common mistake to use just one equals sign in a test. So remember that:

```
x = y;
```

means that x becomes equal to y. But the expression:

```
x==y
```

means a test to see whether x is equal to y.

Choosing the appropriate operator often has to be done with great care. In the program to test whether someone can vote, the appropriate test should probably be:

```
if (age >= 18) cout << "you can vote";
```

Note that it is usually possible to write conditions in either of two ways. The following two program fragments achieve exactly the same result, but use different conditions:

```
cin >> age;
if (age >= 18)
    cout << "you can vote";
else
    cout << "sorry";
cout << "good-bye";
```

achieves the same end as:

```
cin >> age;
if (age < 17)
    cout << "sorry";
else
    cout << "you can vote";
cout << "good-bye";
```

And, or, not

Fairly often in programming we need to test two things at once. Suppose, for example, we want to test whether someone should pay a junior rate for a ticket:

```
if (age>6 && age < 16)
    cout << "junior rate";
```

The double ampersands (&&) mean and.

Brackets can be used to improve the readability of these more complex conditions:

```
if ((age>6) && (age < 16))
    cout << "junior rate";
```

It might be very tempting to write:

```
if (age > 6 && < 18) // error!
```

but this is incorrect – the conditions have to be spelled out in full:

```
if (age > 6 && age < 18) // OK
```

The complete list of these logical operators is:

```
&&   means and
||   means or
!    means not
```

The use of || is illustrated in the following test to see whether a character is a lower case or upper case letter e:

```
char c;

cin >> c;
if (c=='e' || c=='E')
     count++;
```

SELF-TEST QUESTION
Write if statements to test whether someone should get a pension. The rules are:

You get a pension if you are a man and over 65.
If you are a woman you get a pension at age 60

The ! operator gets a lot of use in programming, even though in English the use of a negative can suffer from lack of clarity. Here is an example of the use of not:

```
if (! (age > 18))
     cout << "too young";
```

which can, of course, be written more simply without the not (!) operator.

SELF-TEST QUESTION
Re-write the above if statement without using the not operator.

Nested if statements

Look at the following program fragment:

```
cin >> age;
if (age > 6)
     if (age < 16)
          cout << "junior rate";
     else
          cout << "adult rate";
```

You will see that the second if statement is completely contained within the first. This is called *nesting*. The meaning of this nested code is as follows:

if the age is greater than 6, then the second if is carried out

if the age is not less than 6, then nothing is done (and the statements that follow this fragment are executed)

The overall effect of this piece of program is:

if the age is greater than 6 and less than 16, the rate is the junior rate

if the age is greater than 6 but not less than 16, the rate is the adult rate

if the age is not greater than 6, nothing happens

It is common to see nesting in programs, but a program like this has a complexity which makes it slightly difficult to understand. Often it is possible to write a program more simply using the logical operators. Here, for example, the same result as above is achieved without nesting:

```
cin >> age;
if ((age>6) && (age<16))
    cout << "junior rate";
else
    cout << "adult rate";
```

SELF-TEST QUESTION

Write C++ code to input a salary and determine how much tax someone should pay according to the following rules:

People pay no tax if they earn less than £6000. They pay tax at the rate of 20% on the amount they earn over £5000 but less than £20,000. They pay tax at 90% on any money they earn over £20,000.

You can read more about nesting in the chapter later in this book on programming style.

switch

If you find that you are writing a lot of if statements together, it may be worth re-writing them as a switch statement. For example, suppose we need a piece of program to display a date. Suppose that the day of the week is represented by an integer called day, which has one of the values 1 to 7, representing the days Monday to Sunday. We could write:

```
if (day==1) cout << "Monday";
else if (day==2) cout << "Tuesday";
else if (day==3) cout << "Wednesday";
else if (day==4) cout << "Thursday";
else if (day==5) cout << "Friday";
else if (day==6) cout << "Saturday";
else if (day==7) cout << "Sunday";
```

Notice that we have chosen to write the else words underneath each other. An alternative style would be to indent them, one from the other, so that successive lines would march rightwards across the page.

Now although this piece of coding is fairly neat, clear and well structured, there is an alternative that has the same effect using the switch statement:

```
switch (day)
{
     case 1 : cout << "Monday"; break;
     case 2 : cout << "Tuesday"; break;
     case 3 : cout << "Wednesday"; break;
     case 4 : cout << "Thursday"; break;
     case 5 : cout << "Friday"; break;
     case 6 : cout << "Saturday"; break;
     case 7 : cout << "Sunday"; break;
}
```

This now shows the symmetry of what is to happen more clearly.

The word break means go to the end of the switch statement.

Notice the brackets around the variable that acts as the control for the switch statement. Notice also the colon following each occurrence of the value of the variable. Curly brackets enclose the complete set of options.

More than one statement can follow an option. For example, one of the options could be:

```
case 4 : cout << "Thursday"; cout << endl; break;
```

Several options can be grouped together, like this:

```
switch (day)
{
     case 1: case 2: case 3: case 4: case 5: cout <<
"weekday"; break;
     case 6: case 7: cout << "weekend"; break;
}
```

Another, sometimes useful part of the switch statement is the default option. Suppose, in the above example, that the value of the integer denoting the day of the week is input from the keyboard. Then there is the distinct possibility that the number entered will not be in the range 0 to 7. Any decent program needs to take account of this, in order to prevent something odd happening. The switch statement is very good at dealing with this situation, because we can supply a 'catch-all' or default option that will be invoked if none of the others are valid:

```
switch (day)
{
    case 1 : cout << "Monday"; break;
    case 2 : cout << "Tuesday"; break;
    case 3 : cout << "Wednesday"; break;
    case 4 : cout << "Thursday"; break;
    case 5 : cout << "Friday"; break;
    case 6 : cout << "Saturday"; break;
    case 7 : cout << "Sunday"; break;

    default : cout << "illegal day"; break;
}
```

The switch statement looks very beguiling, but unfortunately it is not as flexible as it could be. Suppose, for example, we want to write a piece of program to output two numbers, with the smallest first, followed by the larger. Using if statements, we have:

```
if (a>b) cout << b << a
else if (b>a) cout << a << b
    else cout "they are equal";
```

We are tempted to re-write this using the switch statement:

```
switch (?) // beware! illegal c++
{
    case a>b : cout << b << a; break;
    case b>a : cout << a << a; break;
    case a==b: cout << "they are equal"; break;
}
```

but this is not allowed because, as indicated by the question mark, switch only works with a single simple variable as its subject – an integer or a character.

Grammar spot

Several aspects of using if statements require care:

- the condition is enclosed in brackets
- within an if, a series of statements is enclosed in curly brackets
- each and every statement within an if must be followed by a semi-colon.

New language elements

```
if
else
==
!=
>
<
>=
<=
&&
||

switch, case, default
```

Programming pitfalls

Don't forget to enclose the condition being tested in an if statement in brackets like this:

```
if (a>b) ...
```

Don't forget that in a test, the test for equality is not = but ==, so:

```
if (a=b) ...
```

will compile correctly and run giving strange results, whereas:

```
if (a==b) ...
```

is probably what you want to write.

You might find that you have written an if statement like this:

```
if (a>18 && <25) ...
```

which is wrong. Instead, the && (meaning and) must link two complete conditions, preferably in brackets for clarity, like this:

```
if ((a>18) && (a<25)) ...
```

Summary

- The if statement allows the programmer to test variables and to take alternative actions depending on the results of the test.
- There are two types of if statement. One has an else part, the other doesn't.

Exercises

1 Write a program to input two numbers and output the larger of the two.
2 Write a program to input any three numbers and output them in increasing numerical size.
3 A well-known holiday company restricts the ages of its clients to the range 18 to 30. Write the code to test whether someone is eligible.
4 Write a program to work out how much a person pays to go to the cinema. The program should input an age and then decide on the following basis:

   under 5, free
   aged 5 to 12, half price
   aged 13 to 54, full price
   aged 55, or over, free

5 A group of people are betting on the outcome of three throws of a die. A person bets £1 on predicting the outcome of the three throws. Write a program that inputs the values of the three throws and displays the winnings according to the following rules:

   all three dice are sixes: win £20
   all three dice are the same (but not sixes): win £10
   any two dice are the same: win £5

CHAPTER 4

Repetition – while *and* for

Introduction

We humans are used to doing things again and again – eating, sleeping, working. Similarly computers routinely perform repetition. Examples are:

- searching files for some desired information
- solving a mathematical equation iteratively, by repeatedly obtaining better and better approximations
- making a graphical figure move on the screen (animation).

Part of the great power of computers arises from their ability to perform repetitions extremely quickly. In the language of programming, a repetition is called a *loop*.

There are three ways in which the C++ programmer can instruct the computer to perform repetition:

- while
- for
- do

Any of these can be used to carry out repetition, but there are differences between them, as we shall see.

We have already seen that a computer obeys a *sequence* of instructions. Now we shall see how to repeat a sequence of instructions a number of times.

while

We are going to illustrate loops by devising some programs to display patterns of asterisks on the screen.

We can output a line of eight asterisks like this:

```
cout <<"********";
```

but another way is to view this as a repetition of the output of a single asterisk. In order to so, we will need a counter. The counter, initially zero, is incremented by one each time a single asterisk is output. We need to repeat the output until the counter reaches the desired total:

```
int counter;
counter = 0;
while (counter < 8)
    {
    cout << "*";
    counter++;
    }
```

This is a while loop. The word while signifies that a repetition is required. The expression in brackets following the word while is the condition for the loop to continue. It says: if the condition is true, the loop is executed. Another way to interpret a while statement is to say that 'such and such is repeated while the condition is true'.

The sequence of statements to be repeated is enclosed in curly brackets and each is followed by a semi-colon.

As a matter of detail, notice that within the loop, we have made use of the shortcut way of adding one to the value of a variable:

```
counter++;
```

The loop repeats with counter equal to 0, 1, 2, ... until it finally has the value 8. The condition is no longer true, so the loop terminates. Eight asterisks have been output.

The above program fragment used the less than (<) operator. This is one of a number of available comparison operators, which are the same as those used in if statements. Here is the complete list of the comparison operators:

>   means greater than
<   means less than
==   means equals
!=   means not equal to
<=   means less than or equal to
>=   means greater than or equal to

The odd one out in this list is the test for equality, which is two equals signs, rather than one. It is a common mistake to use just one equals sign in a test. Great care needs to be taken in making sure that the condition is correct. This is a common cause of errors in programs.

SELF-TEST QUESTION
What would this program fragment do?

```
int counter;
counter = 0;
while (counter <= 8)
```

```
        {
        cout << "*";
        counter++;
        }
```

Another illustration of the use of the while statement is provided by the following example. Suppose we want to use the computer like a desk or pocket calculator to add up a series of numbers. We could write:

```
int sum;
int n1, n2, n3, n4;

sum=0;
cin >> n1;
sum = sum + n1;

cin >> n2;
sum = sum + n1 + n2;

cin >> n3;
sum = sum + n1 + n2 + n3;
```

and so on.

First, the value of sum is made zero. Then the first number is added to it, then the second, etc. This is OK, but it is clumsy. It also assumes that we know in advance how many numbers we are going to add together. On some occasions we might have three numbers, on other occasions 10, or perhaps 6753.

We will change the specification so that the numbers to be added together are followed by the number zero. The program must repeat the adding until zero is input. The sequence to be repeated is:

```
cin >> number;
sum = sum + number;
```

So we surround this sequence with curly brackets and precede it with a while statement:

```
int sum, number;

sum=0;
while (number != 0)
        {
        cin >> number;
        sum = sum + number;
```

```
    }
cout << sum;
```

The pair of symbols '!=' means 'not equal to'. It is one of the available set of comparison operators given above and in Appendix E.

The repetition continues if the condition is true (when the number is non-zero) and ceases when the condition becomes false (when the number is zero).

The above program fragment is beguilingly simple – but it does not work correctly and it needs improving. The reason is that the first time the variable number is tested, it has not been given a value. The value could be anything – even zero, by chance. So we have to give it a well-defined value, like this for example:

```
number=0;
```

This is, however, a clumsy fix. A better solution is to input the first number, before the loop commences:

```
sum=0;
cin >> number;

while (number != 0)
    {
    sum = sum + number;
    cin >> number;
    }
cout << sum;
```

This is the classic solution to this problem. It is a stereotypical structure that can be used in the solution of many similar problems. The general nature of these problems is that information is input and processed a piece at a time until some termination marker.

This problem (and its solution) is typical of those solved using the while loop. We do not know in advance how many repetitions are going to be needed. It could be 10 or 10,000.

This program structure can seem a little strange to the novice programmer. There is the initial input of the first piece of data, which is treated differently from the remainder of the data. Within the loop, first the data is processed and then the (next piece of) data is input. Both these features are counter-intuitive. It needs a little study to become convinced that this structure does indeed match the problem to be solved.

SELF-TEST QUESTION
Alter the above program slightly so that it inputs numbers and adds them together until a negative number is input. The negative number is not part of the total.

for

In the for loop, many of the ingredients of the while loop are bundled up together in the statement itself. Here, for example, is the code to display a row of asterisks on the screen:

```
int count, number_required;

number_required=8;

for (count = 0; count < number_required; count++)
    cout << "*";
```

Within the brackets there are three ingredients, separated by semi-colons:

- an initial statement – what is to be done once before the loop is started
- a condition – what is tested prior to any execution of the loop
- a statement that is carried out just before the end of each repetition.

The condition determines whether the loop is executed or completed:

- if the condition is true, the loop continues
- if the condition is false, the loop ends.

This rule is the same as in the while statement. Similarly, the test is carried out before the loop.

The above loop works as follows. Initially the count is equal to zero. This is less than 8, so the loop is carried out and an asterisk is output. Then the count is incremented to 1. This is still less than 8, so the loop is carried out again. This continues until the final asterisk is output, the count becomes 8 (which is not less than 8) and the loop is over.

If two or more statements are to be repeated, then we need curly brackets around them. This is illustrated in the following program fragment, where a column of asterisks is to be output:

```
int count, number_required;

number_required=8;

for (count = 0; count < number_required; count++)
    {
    cout << "*";
    cout << endl;
    }
```

This example of a for loop is typical. Such loops are normally used when the number of repetitions is known in advance. For example, in the above case, we know how many asterisks are to be displayed.

SELF-TEST QUESTION
Write a program that uses a for statement to input and add together 10 numbers that are input from the keyboard.

SELF-TEST QUESTION
Re-write the above for loop to output asterisks using a while statement instead.

do while

If you use while or for, the test is done at the beginning of the loop. In the do loop, the decision is made at the end of the loop.

Suppose we want a program to input some numbers and add them up, prompting the user each time for a number. Using a do loop we can write this as:

```
integer total, number;
char reply;

do
    {
    cout << "give me a number please" << endl;
    cin >> number;
    total=total+number;
    cout << "any more?" << endl;
    cin >> reply;
    }
while (reply != 'n')

cout << total;
```

As with while and for loops, the condition determines whether or not the loop is repeated:

- if the condition is true, the loop is repeated
- if the condition is false, the loop is not repeated.

Because the test is at the end of the loop, the repetition is always performed once, at least. In contrast, loops constructed using while or if may not be executed at all, depending on circumstances. Expressed another way, a while or a for loop may repeat zero times, but a do loop is always carried out at least once.

And, or, not

On occasions, the condition that controls a loop is more complex and we need the and, or and not operators. We met these in Chapter 3 on decisions using the if statement. The list of these logical operators is:

&&   means and
|| means or
!   means not

Suppose, for example, that we are writing a program to carry out a dialogue with the user of the computer. As is common, we want the user to respond to a question with either the reply 'y' or the reply 'n'. If the user responds with something other than either of these two, then we want to go on prompting the user.

```
do
    {
    cout << "Do you want to delete the file?";
    cin >> character;
    }
while ( character != 'y' && character != 'n');
```

The pair of symbols && mean 'and'. This loop will repeat until the character that is input is either 'y' or 'n'. So it will continue while the character is not 'y' and not 'n'.

If you use these operators in loops, your programs can become quite complicated. Indeed, the condition in the program fragment above is not the most obvious. Ways of avoiding complication are described in Chapter 20 on program style.

SELF-TEST QUESTION
Write a program to input numbers from the keyboard and add them together. The sequence of numbers ends either with the number 0 or the number 999.

Nested loops

A nested loop is where there is a loop within a loop. Suppose, for example, we want to output the following:

```
bbbbb
bbbbb
bbbbb
```

which is a crude block of apartments! Each line is repeated. But also, within each line, the letter 'b' is repeated. So the loops are nested:

```
for (line = 0; line < 3; line++)
    {
    for (character = 0; character < 5; character++)
        {
        cout << "b";
        }
    cout << endl;
    }
```

and you will see that both the indentation and the curly brackets help considerably in understanding the program.

Programming pitfalls

Be very careful with the conditions in looping statements. It is a very common error to make a loop finish early or else to repeat too many times.

Grammar spot

When two or more statements are to be repeated, they must be enclosed in curly brackets. Each statement is followed by a semi-colon.
In the while, for and do loop, the condition is enclosed in brackets.

New language elements

```
while
for
do
```

Summary

- A repetition in programming is called a loop.
- There are three ways of instructing the computer to loop: while, for and do.
- Use while when you do not know in advance how many repetitions will have to be performed.
- Use for when you do know in advance how many repetitions will have to be performed.
- Use do sparingly, when a loop is to be performed at least once.

Exercises

1 Write a program to display the numbers 1 to 100.
2 Write a program that inputs a series of integers and finds their sum, the largest number, the smallest number and their average value. The numbers end with the number zero.
3 Write a program to input eight numbers and display their sum.
4 Write a program that first inputs the number of numbers that follow. Then the program inputs and adds up the numbers. So, for example, the program inputs the number 5, followed by five numbers.
5 Write a program that adds up the numbers 0 to 39 using a loop. Check that it has obtained the right answer by using the formula for the sum of the numbers 0 to n:

$$n(n+1)/2$$

6 Write a program to display the following (sawtooth) pattern on the screen:

```
S
SS
SSS
SSSS
SSSSS
S
SS
SSS
SSSS
SSSSS
```

7 Write a program to display a multiplication table, such as young children use. For example, the table for numbers up to 6 is:

	1	2	3	4	5	6
1	1	2	3	4	5	6
2	2	4	6	8	10	12
3	3	6	9	12	15	18
4	4	8	12	16	20	24
5	5	10	15	20	25	30
6	6	12	18	24	30	36

The program should produce a table of any size, specified by an integer input from the keyboard.
8 The Fibonaccii series is the series of numbers:

1 1 2 3 5 8 13 ...

Each number (except for the first two) is the sum of the previous two numbers. The series is supposed to govern growth in plants. Write a program to create and display the first ten Fibonaccii numbers.

9 Write a program to calculate and display the series:

$$1 - 1/2 + 1/3 - 1/4 + \ldots$$

until a term is less than 0.0001.

10 Nim is a game played with matchsticks (unused or used, it does not matter). It doesn't matter how many matches there are. The matches are put into three piles. Again, it doesn't matter how many matches there are in each pile. Each player goes in turn. A player can remove any number of matches from any one pile, but only one pile. A player must remove at least one match. The winner is the person who causes the other player to take the last match. Write a program to allow two players to play Nim.

CHAPTER 5
Calculations

Introduction

This chapter brings together all the information you need to write programs that carry out calculations. Some of this information has been described already in earlier chapters.

Calculations arise in many programs – not just programs that carry out mathematical, scientific or engineering calculations. In information systems, calculations arise in payrolls, accountancy and forecasting. In graphics, calculations are necessary to scale and move objects as they appear on the screen.

int or float?

There are two ways of representing numbers in C++: integers (int) and floating point (float) numbers. An integer is a whole number, like the number 3 or 365. Floating point numbers have a decimal point in them, like 1234.9 or 0.0007.

Integers are held exactly in a computer. The snag is that the range of numbers that can be held in an integer variable (of the type int) is limited. A typical range for integers that can be represented as int is −32,768 to +32,767. Any numbers bigger than 32,767 or smaller than −32,768 simply cannot be represented as int. The available range of numbers differs from computer to computer – there is no standardization here. You will have to check the manual for your C++ system to find out the possible range of integers available to you.

The range of floating point numbers (float in C++) that can be held is much greater than for integers. Typical values are 10^{-37} to 10^{+37} (both positive and negative). Again, you will have to check the manual for your system to find out the relevant values for your system. The snag with floating point numbers is that they are only represented to a particular degree of accuracy – a number of digits of precision. Typical values are six digits. Floating point numbers are sometimes called *real* numbers in the jargon of computing.

Which to choose – int or float? The answer is usually determined by the problem to be solved. Here are some examples:

a salary	int
a product number	int
dimensions of a room	float

Declaration, assignment and input/output

Integers and floating point numbers are declared as shown in the following examples:

```
int salary;
float length;
```

A variable can be given a value in an assignment statement like this:

```
salary = 100000;
length = 12.45;
```

Input and output look like this:

```
cin >> salary;
salary = salary + 1000;
cout << salary;

cin >> length >> breadth;
area = length*breadth;
cout << area;
```

Calculation

The usual arithmetic operators are provided in C++ to carry out calculations – addition, subtraction, multiplication and division. With floating point numbers, it is straightforward:

+   means add
−   means subtract
*   means multiply
/   means divide

Carrying out division on integers is special. Dividing integers gives rise to an integer result and a remainder. So two operators are provided. The result of such a division is then truncated to give an integer, so that:

5 divided by 2 gives 2 remainder 1

The operators for integer arithmetic are:

+   means add
−   means subtract

```
*    means multiply
/    means divide and give the quotient (truncated)
%    means divide and give the remainder
```

There are rules (see below) that clarify the meanings of expressions like:

```
a * b + c - d / e
```

but it is much clearer to insert brackets:

```
(a * (b + c)) - (d / e)
```

Mixing integers with floating point numbers in calculations needs special attention and is described later.

As an example of a calculation, consider the calculation of the roots of a quadratic equation, $ax^2 + bx + c = 0$:

```
float a, b, c;
float d, r1, r2;

cin >> a >> b >> c;
d= (b*b) - (4.0*a*c);
r1= (-b+sqrt(d))/(2.0*a);
r2= (-b-sqrt(d))/(2.0*a);
```

where sqrt is a standard mathematical function, described below.

Operator precedence

If you see an expression like this in a program:

```
a * b + c - d / e
```

then it is not clear – unless you know the rules – what it means. It could mean, do the multiplication first, then the addition, etc. This would be a left-to-right rule.

It does matter which order you use for interpretation, because, for example:

```
(3/4) + 1
```

is not the same as:

```
3/(4+1)
```

The safe way to handle the situation is to put brackets in expressions to clarify them. The alternative is to learn the *precedence rules*. Precedence rules say that some operators have higher importance (precedence) than others. Thus:

```
*  /    have highest precedence and are done first
+  -    have lowest precedence and are done last
```

Thus 3/4+1 actually means (3/4)+1.

If two operators have equal precedence, then the expression is calculated left to right. Thus 3/4*2 means (3/4)*2.

SELF-TEST QUESTION
What do these mean?

```
2+3+4
2-3+4
2*3/4
2/3*4
a * b + c - d / e
```

Standard mathematical functions

It is very common in mathematical, scientific or engineering programs to need certain functions like sine, cosine and log. In C++, these are provided in one of the libraries – the mathematics library. To use one of the functions, the include statement must appear at the head of the program:

```
#include <math.h>
```

and thereafter we can use the functions from the library like this:

```
y=sqrt(y);
```

which calculates the square root of the parameter.

Some of the functions in the mathematics library usually present with a C++ system are given below. The parameters must be floating point numbers.

```
cos (x)     cosine of the angle x, expressed in radians
sin (x)     sine of the angle x, expressed in radians
tan (x)     tangent of the angle x, expressed in radians
fabs (x)    the absolute value of x, sometimes written |x|
log (x)     natural logarithm of x (to the base e)
log10 (x)   logarithm of x to base 10
```

```
sqrt (x)    the positive square root of x
pow (x, y)  x raised to the power of y, xy
```

Comparison

A typical example of comparing numbers is in a program, again, to calculate the roots of a quadratic. Once the so-called discriminant has been calculated, we should test to see whether there are imaginary roots:

```
d= (b*b) − (4.0*a*c);
if (d<0)
    cout << "imaginary roots";
else
    {
    r1= (−b+sqrt(d))/(2.0*a);
    r2= (−b-sqrt(d))/(2.0*a);
    cout << r1 << r2;
    }
```

Iteration

It is quite common in numerical programming to write iterations – loops that continue searching for a solution to an equation, until the solution is found to sufficient accuracy.

As an example of using iteration, there is a formula for the sine of an angle:

$$\sin(x) = x - x^3/3! + x^5/5! - x^7/7! + \ldots$$

(If we need the sine of an angle in a program, we don't need to use this formula, because sine is available as a standard function.)

We can see that each term is derived from the previous term by multiplying by:

$$-x^2/(n+1)(n+2)$$

so we can construct a loop that iterates until the new term is less than some acceptable figure, say 0.0001:

```
float sin, x, term;

sin=0;
term=x;
n=1;
```

```
while (fabs(term) >= 0.0001)
    {
    sin=sin+term;
    term=-term*x*x/((n+1)*(n+2));
    n=n+2;
    }
```

in which the standard function `fabs` (mentioned above) calculates the absolute value of its parameter.

Converting between integers and floating point numbers

We have seen that C++ distinguishes between integer and floating point numbers and that we have to be careful with statements and expressions that mix the two. Sometimes we want to be completely explicit and deliberate. C++ provides functions explicitly to convert from `float` to `int` and vice versa.
So:

```
int i;
float x;

float (i)
```

converts the integer i to a floating point number, and:

```
int (x)
```

converts x to an integer, by chopping off (truncating) the fractional part of the number. Thus:

```
int(3.7) is 3
```

Summary

- Computer programs are typically used to carry out calculations in mathematics, statistics, engineering and science.
- Numbers can be represented as either integers or floating point numbers. These provide different ranges and precision.
- Input, output, calculations, comparison and loops are all readily possible.
- Standard library functions provide the common mathematical functions, for example sine.

Exercises

1   Write a program to input two numbers, representing the measurements (length and breadth) of a room, and display the area of the room.

2   A phone call costs 4 pence per minute. Write a program that inputs the duration of a phone call, expressed in hours, minutes and seconds, and displays the cost of the phone call in pence.

3   Write a program to input a measurement expressed in feet and inches and convert the measurement to centimetres. (There are 12 inches in a foot. One inch is 2.54 centimetres.)

4   The sum of the integers 1 to n is given by the formula:

$$n(n+1)/2$$

Write a program that inputs a value for n and calculates the sum two ways – first by using the formula and second by adding up the numbers using a loop.

5   Check out the random number generator function (Appendix C). Key in the following program that displays eight random numbers and check that the numbers do, indeed, look random. Are you convinced that it works OK?

```
#include <stdlib.h>
#include <iostream.h>

int main (void)
{
    int count;

    for ( count = 1; count <= 8; count++)
    cout << (rand () % 13) + 1;
}
```

6   The value of e^x can be calculated by summing the series:

$$e^x = 1 + x + x^2/2! + x^3/3! + \ldots$$

Write a program to input a value of x and calculate e^x to a certain degree of accuracy.

7   Write a program that carries out a tax calculation. The tax is zero on the first £10,000, but is 33% on any amount over that amount. Write the program to input a salary in £ and calculate the tax payable. Watch out for errors when you perform the calculation – the answer needs to be accurate to the nearest penny!

8   The area of a triangle with sides a, b, c is:

$$area = sqrt(s(s-a)(s-b)(s-c))$$

where:

$$s = (a + b + c)/2$$

Write a program that inputs the three values for the sides of a triangle and uses this formula to calculate the area. Your program should first check that the three lengths specified do indeed form a triangle.

9 The square root of a number can be calculated iteratively as shown below. Write a program to do this for a number input from the keyboard.

The first approximation to the square root of x is $x/2$

Then successive approximations are given by the formula:

next_approximation = $(\text{last\_approximation}^2 - x)/2 + \text{last\_approximation}$

CHAPTER 6

Character data

Introduction

Character data has already been mentioned in earlier chapters of this book. This chapter brings together into one place the information about using character data.

Character data is text – letters, punctuation marks and all the other characters on the keyboard. This chapter explains how to write programs to process character data. Such data might typically be names, addresses, descriptions of products – anything that is not numbers. If you were going to write a program to analyze the works of Shakespeare, you would need to use character data. If you were going to write a word processor, you would need character data.

The facilities for character data in C++ can seem a bit disappointing, particularly if you are used to some other programming languages. A variable that holds character data will only hold *one single character*. It will *not* hold a word or a string of characters. This means that writing programs to handle character data can be hard work.

Although the basic facilities for character handling are fairly limited, C++ provides more sophisticated facilities for groups of characters called strings. These are the subject of Chapter 15.

Declaring character data

In C++, character variables are declared like this:

```
char c, character;
```

Each such variable can hold just one character. So we can picture a character variable as a box in main memory, with a name attached to it:

The permissible characters that can be held in a character variable include anything that is available on the keyboard. This means:

lower case letters
upper case letters
punctuation marks . , ! ? : ;
other exotic characters like ^
mathematical symbols like + − * /
the digits 0 to 9
spaces

It is important to understand the difference between a number, say 7, and a digit, say 7. The fact is that there is no difference − except in the way that they are processed by a program.

If the key depression is input into an integer variable, then it is treated as an integer. Thereafter, it can be used in calculations, like this:

```
int integer;

cin >> integer;
integer = integer + 45;
```

Alternatively, if the same key depression is input into a character variable, then it is treated as a character. This time, it can't be used as an integer and it can't be used in calculations.

```
char character;

cin >> character;
character = character + 42; // is meaningless and illegal
```

Input/output

We can use cin to input a character. The coding:

```
char c;

cin >> c;
```

inputs a *single* character from the keyboard and places it in the character variable c. Any spaces and newlines in the input are ignored, or skipped. If you want to write a program that explicitly takes account of spaces, then you have to use a different function, like this:

```
char c;
c = cin.get();
```

which inputs the next character from the keyboard, whatever it is.

As with integers, we can use cout to output the value of a character variable to the screen:

```
char c;

cout << c;
```

So we can write a little piece of program that inputs a single character from the keyboard and echoes it to the screen:

```
char c;

cin >> c;
cout << c;
```

Any newlines or spaces that are input will be ignored by this piece of program.

SELF-TEST QUESTION
Write a fragment of program that inputs a date in the format:

28/12/2005

so that the three numbers are input into three integer variables called day, month and year.

Assigning values

A character variable can be given a value in an assignment statement, like this:

```
c = 'y';
```

Notice that the single character is enclosed in single quotes, different from the double quotes used when outputting text:

```
cout << "hello";
```

Testing characters

Character variables can easily be tested in if and while statements.

For example, suppose we have input a character into the variable one_char. We can test to see whether it is the letter e like this:

```
if (one_char == 'e')
    cout << "yes - it is e";
```

Or to input characters, one by one, until a full stop is reached:

```
cin >> one_char;
while (one_char != '.')
    cin >> one_char;
```

In summary, the usual comparison operators can be used with characters:

== means equals
!= means not equal to

and conditions can be combined using the logical operators, so that, for example, we could test a character to see whether it is e or E like this:

```
if (one_char == 'e' || one_char =='E')
    cout << "yes - it is e";
```

Or to input until a full stop or a semi-colon is reached:

```
cin >> one_char;
while (one_char != '.' && one_char != ';')
    cin >> one_char;
```

SELF-TEST QUESTION
Write a fragment of program to test whether a particular character is a vowel or not.

Alphabetical order

It is fairly common to want to sort data into alphabetical order, and often computers are used to do this. To write such a program we would need to compare pairs of words. In C++, because character handling is done a character at a time, we need to compare two individual characters to see whether they are in alphabetical order. This is done using the usual comparison operators:

```
if (this_one < that_one)
    cout << this_one << "comes before" << that_one;
else
    cout << that_one << "comes before" << this_one;
```

When used with character data, therefore, the comparison operators have the following meanings:

<   means comes alphabetically before
>   means comes alphabetically after

Finally, if we input a character and want to test to see whether it is a letter, we could make use of a horrendously long collection of if statements. Instead we can make use of:

```
cin >> c;
if(('A' <= c && c <= 'Z') || ('a' <= c && c <= 'z'))
    cout << c << "is a letter";
```

This relies on the fact (usually hidden) that C++ actually represents characters as numbers, and these numbers follow on from one another – they are consecutive.

Summary

- A character variable holds just one character.
- Characters can be input and output from the keyboard using cin and cout.
- Character variables can be tested in if and while statements.
- Character variables can be tested to see if they are in alphabetical order.

Exercises

1 Write a program to find out the percentage occurrence of the letter e in a piece of text entered from the keyboard and terminated by a full-stop character.
2 Write a program to find the average word length in a piece of text, entered from the keyboard and terminated by a full stop. As a first program, simplify the text so that there is only one space or newline between each word. Later you might like to make things more complicated by allowing there to be several spaces between words.
3 Write a program that inputs two characters and outputs them in alphabetical order.

CHAPTER 7
Functions

Introduction

Functions are the way of constructing what might be complex programs from small, simple components. Nearly every program that you see or write that is more than about 50 lines in length consists of a number of functions. Programs that are large – 20 pages or more – always consist of functions. Thus functions are an important and vital element of programming.

Functions are about doing things in manageable pieces. Functions are about coping with complexity by divide and rule. Functions are about selecting various tasks and delegating them.

Every artefact that humans have created consists of pieces. A car consists of a body, an engine, a transmission system and so on. Each subsystem carries out a distinct task which contributes towards the overall job that the car has to do. Each subsystem consists, in turn, of further subsystems. The same is true of office blocks, washing machines and bridges.

In this chapter we introduce the concept of functions, using several examples.

There are several different ways in which functions communicate information (data) between each other. This is the subject of the next few chapters.

Simple functions

Look at the following simple program:

```
int main (void)
{
int a, b, s;

cout << "Hello. How are you?" << endl;
cin >> a >> b;
s = a+b;
cout << s;
cout << "Good-bye. Thank you" << endl;
}
```

There are three rather separate parts to this program – the greeting, the calculation and the farewell. Using functions we can separate the three elements. The main function can delegate a task to another function. Rather than doing everything itself and having too much to do, some of the work can be given to someone else. This generally promotes simplicity and clarity.

We can re-write the above program like this:

```
int main (void)
{
int a, b, s;

void hello (void); // this is a prototype - see later
void bye (void); // this is a prototype - see later

hello();
cin >> a >> b;
s = a+b;
cout << s;
bye();
}

void hello (void)
{
cout << "Hello. How are you?" << endl;
}

void bye (void)
{
cout << "Good-bye. Thank you" << endl;
}
```

We now have three functions – the function main and the two functions that main uses (hello and bye). The notation:

```
hello();
```

is termed a function *call*. It instructs the computer to go off to the function named hello, carry out the instructions within the function and then return. The return is always to the statement after the function call, which in this case is the cin.

Functions are a way of packaging a subtask in a neat bundle. The bundle is given a name by the programmer, and thereafter it can be used simply by giving its name.

When a function is called, the flow of control goes into the function. When the instructions within the function are complete, the computer returns and executes the instruction immediately after the call.

Most programs are constructed as a collection of functions. A function will be as long as it needs to be – anything from one line to 50 lines. The paramount guideline governing the length of a function is clarity.

There are three elements to using a function:

- the function call
- the definition of the function
- the function prototype (see below).

The definition of a function has a header, followed by a body.

The header includes the name of the function, together with some other information that we will look at in the next two chapters. For now, just copy what you see in the examples.

The body of a function is sandwiched between an open curly bracket, {, and a close curly bracket, }. The body consists of the declarations of any data that the function is going to use, followed by the actions that the function is going to carry out. As usual, each statement is followed by a semi-colon.

SELF-TEST QUESTION

A program is about to be written and it has been recognized that there is a need to output a line of dashes to the screen several times during the execution of the program. Write a function to provide such a service. Give the function the name Dashes.

Function names

The programmer chooses the names for functions. C++ allows for a wide variety of names and, in fact, the rules for function names are the same as for variable names. There's plenty of scope for choosing a good name because:

- names consist of letters, digits and underlines
- names can be as long as you like

provided that:

- a name starts with a letter
- a name is unique somewhere in its first 32 characters.

These rules are provided for reference in Appendix D.

The advice on names is to make them as meaningful as possible in order to promote clarity in your programs. A name like do_it is meaningless; input_data is better; input_prices is better still.

Be careful, because the names Doug and doug are different – the difference between upper and lower case *does* matter.

SELF-TEST QUESTION

Which of these are valid function names?

add, convert_to_integer, Input_Data, main, function_2

Prototypes

One of the rules of the C++ language is that everything must be declared before it is used. We have already seen that variables have to be declared before they are used; the same is true of functions.

If a function is going to use (call) another function whose name is (say) funky, then:

```
void funky (void);
```

must appear at the start of the function, usually before the variable declarations. This is called a *function prototype*. It announces the fact that the function is going to be called. It is like someone saying 'at some point later on, I am going to use the lift'. Notice that it is followed by a semi-colon.

If a prototype is omitted, the compiler issues one of its obscure error messages.

The term prototype is, on the face of it, a bit strange. A prototype usually means a preliminary or trial version of something that is constructed prior to the development of the real thing. This isn't really the meaning in the context of C++. It's rather more like an exemplar, pattern or template that tells the compiler (and us human readers) some things about a function that is going to be used.

SELF-TEST QUESTION
Write the prototype for the function Dashes that was the subject of an earlier question.

include **and the libraries**

Now is a good time to explain the nature of the include statements that appear at the top of any C++ program, like this:

```
#include <iostream.h>
```

This instruction directs the compiler to go to a system file called iostream.h. In the file is information about the library of functions provided for input and output, including cin and cout. Part of this information is the prototypes of the functions. This makes it unnecessary for the programmer to code a prototype for a library function.

Library functions are important in C++ programming – in fact in programming in any language. Libraries save us lots of work, because usually all of the things that we want to do frequently have already been written (as functions) and are in the library. We shall meet some of these library functions in later chapters of this book. The most popular functions provide input/output, mathematical calculations, string handling and file handling. There is a summary in Appendix B.

A case study

In order to illustrate the use of functions in a program of a more realistic size, we will examine a program that provides the user with information on a variety of musical performers. If we consider all the performers – world-wide, over 50 years, all musical tastes – there is an enormous number of them, and the program is potentially huge.

We will begin the program by asking about the time period:

```
int main (void)
{
char answer;

cout << "post 1990?";
cin >> answer;
if (answer == 'y')
    new artist();
else
    old_artist();
};
```

To remind you, the notation:

```
new_artist();
```

instructs the computer to go off to the function new_artist, carry out the instructions within the function and then return.

The function new_artist looks like:

```
void new_artist (void)
{
char reply;

cout << "female?";
cin >> reply;
if (reply=='y')
    female();
else
    male();
};
```

and, in turn:

```
void female (void)
{
cout << "the only new female performer is";
cout << "Tina Turner";
};
```

We could continue the development of this program. It is potentially a very large program consisting of tens of functions, each dealing with a part of the information about performers.

SELF-TEST QUESTION
Write a function called male to fit in with the above program and display some information about your favourite male artist.

SELF-TEST QUESTION
Write prototypes for the functions given above.

Local data

When a function needs variables to carry out its task, they are usually declared just inside the function. Examples in the above program are the variables answer and reply. They are called *local variables* or *local data* because they are used only within the function. Indeed such variables cannot be referred to by any other function – they are entirely secret. Any reference to a local variable by another function gives a compilation error.

Thus the variable reply in function new, for example, is completely personal to that function. No other function can refer to reply or use it in any way. It's like individual, separate work space that is the exclusive territory of that function.

The data declared at the top of function main (the variable called answer) is also local data. It is individual to main, and cannot be referred to by any other function.

Grammar spot

A function involves three components:

- a prototype
- the function definition
- one or more function calls.

The function definition consists of a function header, followed by the function body. The function body is enclosed in curly brackets.

Each statement in the function body is followed by a semi-colon.

Function prototypes and function calls are followed by a semi-colon, but function headers are not. Neither is an include statement.

Programming pitfalls

A function prototype and a function call have a semi-colon; a function header does not.

Suppose you want to use (call) a function named elephant. If you write:

```
elephant;
```

the call will not work (although there will be no protest from the compiler). Instead you must write:

```
elephant();
```

Summary

- Functions are the way to simplify programming by constructing programs from small, manageable pieces
- Before a function is used, a prototype declaration must specify its name and various other information.
- Local data is the collection of variables that is declared inside a function. This data is available to this function only.

Exercises

1 A song has three verses, each followed by a chorus. Write a program to display the song. Use separate functions for each verse and one function for the chorus.
2 Add more functions to the program (above) that give information on musical performers.
3 Using a pencil or a ball-point pen, follow the flow of execution through the musical performers' program. Check that you are clear as to the way control flows into a function and then back to where the function was called from.

CHAPTER 8

Functions with parameters

Introduction

We saw in the previous chapter how easy and desirable it is to construct a program from a group of functions. In this chapter, we look at

- how data can be sent to a function so that it can be worked upon
- how any data can be sent back from a function.

Passing parameters to a function

Suppose we want to construct a function that outputs asterisks to the screen. We intend this function to be part of a program that is going to output patterns of asterisks to the screen, like this:

```
*
**
***
****
```

In thinking about the design of this program, we decide that it would be useful to have a function that would display a variable number of asterisks. We would use (call) the function like this:

```
line (7);
```

The pieces of data sent to the function are called parameters. There is one parameter in this example which says how many asterisks are to be displayed.

This function, called line, is a very useful one because we can use it to display any number of repetitions of asterisks. In the program we are actually working on, we can use a variable as the parameter:

```
line (count);
```

which again shows how flexible the function is.

If we are going to employ this function, we will need a prototype:

```
void line (int);
```

which spells out:

- the name of the function
- how many parameters there are (one in this case)
- the type of the parameter (an integer in this case).

The function itself looks like this:

```
void line (int number)
{
    int count;
    for (count=0; count < number; count++)
        cout << '*';
    cout << endl;
}
```

SELF-TEST QUESTION
Write a program that uses the function line, given above, to output the following pattern:

```
*
**
***
****
```

If a function does not use any parameters the word void is used instead of the list of parameters, like this:

```
void function_needs_nothing (void)
```

We will now generalize the function that we constructed so that a call on it looks like this:

```
line ( '*', 7);
```

and it will display any number of any character. There are now two parameters. The first parameter is the character that is to be displayed. In this case it is an asterisk. The second parameter says how many asterisks are to be displayed.

In a different program, we could use the function like this:

```
line ( '%', 20);
```

to display 20 percentage symbols. Now the coding of the function is:

```
void line (char c, int number)
{
     int count;
     for (count=0; count < number; count++)
          cout << c;
     cout << endl;
}
```

and the prototype is:

```
void line (char c, int number);
```

SELF-TEST QUESTION

Write a program that uses the function line, given above, to output the following pattern:

```
*
* *
* * *
* * * *
```

Using parameters

We have now constructed a function that has the following prototype:

```
void line(char c, int number);
```

One of the great joys of functions is that we can call a function with any parameters that we like. Here are some sample, valid calls on function line:

```
line ('@', 20);

line ('a', 129);

int how_many;
char one_char;

cin >> one_char;
cin >> how_many;
line (one_char, how_many);
```

When you call a function, the names of the parameters do not have to match the names of the parameters in the prototype or in the function header. This means that functions are general purpose and very flexible.

All that we have to do when we use a function is to ensure that:

- we have got the function name right
- we have the required number of parameters (two for the function line)
- the parameters are in the right order.

These are very easy rules to follow.

SELF-TEST QUESTION
What is the effect of writing this call on the function line?

```
line (22, '+');
```

Passing parameters back from a function

So far, we have looked at parameters that were used by a function – but not changed or given values. Now we complete the story about parameters.

Suppose we want a function to find the larger of two numbers. We pass the two numbers as parameters to the function for it to use. We also want the function to pass some data back to the user of the function, namely the value of the number that is the larger. A call on the function is:

```
larger (a, b, L);
```

where a and b are the two numbers and L is the larger. So far, nothing is any different from what we have seen before. The difference is in the function itself (and in the prototype):

```
void larger (int x, int y, int & B)
{
     if (x>y)
          B=x;
     else
          B=y;
}
```

The small, but significant, point of interest is the ampersand (&) before the parameter name in the function header. The rule is that any parameter whose value is affected by a function must have an ampersand in front of it in the function header. The same is true of the prototype:

```
void larger (int , int , int & );
```

SELF-TEST QUESTION
Write a program that inputs two integers, uses the function larger (given above) and outputs the result obtained by the function.

As another example, consider a function that inputs a word (a series of letters) from the keyboard and returns as a parameter the length of the word. A call on the function is:

```
read_word (size);
```

and the function definition is:

```
void read_word (int & length)
{
      char letter;

      length=0;
      cin >> letter;
      while (letter != ',')
          {
          length++;
          cin >> letter;
          }
}
```

Sometimes a parameter is used to communicate some data both to a function and also from the function. In a sense, it is both input to and output from the function. As an example, consider a function that converts a length measured in inches into centimetres. A program fragment with a call to this function is:

```
float length;

cin >> length;
convert_to_centimetres (length);

cout << length;
```

and the function definition is:

```
void convert_to_centimetres (float & length)
{
      length=length*2.54;
}
```

with an ampersand to indicate that the value of the parameter will be affected by the function.

SELF-TEST QUESTION
Write a function that adds one to the value of its parameter (an integer).

SELF-TEST QUESTION
Write a function that converts a time measured in minutes and seconds into the same time measured in seconds.

Value and reference parameters

We have seen that parameters are the mechanism by which data is communicated between functions. One function, the calling function, calls another function, the called function. Data that is to be communicated is of three types:

1   Data to be passed to the called function for it to act upon. The called function uses the data, but does not change it. In the jargon of programming, this is termed a *value* parameter.
2   Data that is created by the called function for the calling function to use. In the jargon, this is called a *reference* parameter. This type of parameter must be preceded by an ampersand (&) in the function prototype and in the function header.
3   Data that is passed to the called function, to be changed by the called function and passed back for use by the calling function. In the jargon, this is also called a *reference* parameter, and must be preceded by an ampersand (&) in the function prototype and in the function header.

SELF-TEST QUESTION
Explain why functions are useful in programming.

Summary

- Data is passed to and from functions as parameters.
- Parameters appear in the prototype, the function call and in the function definition.
- A parameter that is changed by a function must be decorated with an ampersand (&) in the function header (and prototype).
- If a function does not use parameters, the word void appears instead of the parameter list in the function prototype and the function header.

Exercises

1 Write a program that makes the most use of functions to display a series of
squares on the screen. The number of squares and the size of each square
(height and breadth) are inputs to the program.

```
* * * * *
*       *
*       *
* * * * *
* * * * *
*       *
*       *
* * * * *
* * * * *
*       *
*       *
* * * * *
```

2 It is quite common for a program to request a reply from the user of the
program which is either the character 'y' (short for yes) or the character 'n'
(for no). Any other response is invalid. Write a function that inputs a
character from the keyboard and checks that the character is either y or n. If
some other character is input, the function outputs an error message and
requests further input. This continues until a valid character is input, which is
returned as a parameter to the user of the function.

CHAPTER 9

Functions that return values

Introduction

If you remember your elementary mathematics, you may recall using mathematical functions like sine, cosine and log. You may remember seeing expressions like sin(30°), meaning the sine of the angle 30 degrees. In this notation, the function sine is applied to the parameter 30. We think of the expression sin(30°) as having a value – in this case 0.5.

In C++ we can write and use functions that allow us to use this same notation for functions. So, for example, we can construct a function whose name is bigger that gives the bigger value of its parameters. A call on the function, like this:

```
bigger (4,5)
```

gives the value 5. We would use a call on a function like this as part of an expression, like this:

```
cout << bigger (4,5);
```

or in an assignment:

```
very_big = largest (34, 67) + largest (42, 64);
```

Returning the value

Consider, as an illustration, a function that calculates the square of an integer. As usual, we will pass the value of the integer to the function as a parameter. But we will return the answer as the value of the function. We will use the function like this:

```
int x, y;

cin >> x;
y = square(x);
cout << y;
```

You will see that the way in which the function is called is very different from what we have seen before. It is on the right hand side of an assignment statement. Once the value of the function square has been obtained, it is assigned to the variable called y. The function call appears as part of an expression. We could use the function call as part of any other expression, for example:

```
if (square(x) > 1000) cout << "the answer is very large";
```

We need a function prototype, as always:

```
int square (int);
```

which now describes the type of the value that is returned by the function (in this case an integer). The function itself is:

```
int square (int n)
{
    return (n*n);
}
```

The `return` statement is a C++ word. It signifies that the function has completed its work and describes the value that is to be returned. The value to be returned from the function is placed in brackets after the word `return`.

As another example, we will look at a function mentioned earlier, whose name is bigger, which calculates the bigger of its two parameters. So bigger (23, 56) returns the value 56.

The function header is:

```
int bigger (int one, int two)
```

and, as ever when constructing functions, writing the function header is a good place to start because it clarifies what the function is going to act on – the parameters.

Now we go on to write the complete function:

```
int bigger (int one, int two)
{
    int B;

    if (one > two)
        B=one;
    else
        B=two;
    return (B);
}
```

As you can see, the function uses a local variable called B and uses a simple if statement to find out which of the two numbers is the greater.

We can now use the function:

```
int first, second;

cin >> first;
cin >> second;
cout << bigger (first, second);
```

One of the good things about using functions that return values is that you can use them together in expressions. For example, suppose we need to find the biggest of three numbers a, b, and c. To accomplish this, we can do this:

```
cout << bigger (a, bigger (b, c));
```

Here bigger is first called with parameters b and c. It returns the larger of these two. Then bigger is called again, this time with its first parameter equal to a and its second parameter equal to the value that bigger just returned.

If a function does not return a value, then the word void precedes the function name in the function header, like this:

```
void function_returns_nothing (int number)
```

Return value or parameter?

There are two alternative mechanisms for passing back a value from a function to its user (caller):

- passing back a parameter
- passing back a value of the function.

We will illustrate the difference by writing a function in two different ways – once returning the value as a parameter and once returning the value as the value of the function (using return). The example is a function that adds together the values of two integers. We will give the function the name add.

First we will use the approach that uses parameters exclusively. The three parameters are the two numbers to be added and the result of the addition. The function prototype is:

```
void add (int x, int y, int & ans)
```

Notice the ampersand (&) before the third parameter, to indicate that this parameter is going to be changed by the function. The function can be called like this:

```
add (3, 4, sum);
```

Now the function itself:

```
void add (int x, int y, int & ans)
{
    ans = x+y;
}
```

The alternative approach is to use only two parameters because the answer is to be returned as the value of the function. The function prototype is:

```
int add (int x, int y)
```

and a typical call on the function is:

```
sum = add (3, 4);
```

The function itself is:

```
int add (int x, int y)
{
    return (x+y);
}
```

Which is better? The answer is that it is largely a question of style. You simply may prefer to call a function using the functional style (as part of an expression) as shown above.

Obviously, if you have several values to pass back from a function, only one of them can be passed back as the value of the function, so you have to use parameters.

SELF-TEST QUESTION
Write a function called add_one that adds one to the value of an integer that is supplied to the function as a parameter. Write the function in two different ways – once returning the value as a parameter and once returning the value as the value of the function (using return).

To summarize, there are three mechanisms for passing data to and from a function:

1   Value parameter – to pass data to a function. The parameter will not and cannot be changed by the function.
2   Reference parameter – to pass data to a function that will change it, or to pass from the function data that the function has created. A reference

parameter must have an ampersand alongside it in the prototype and in the function header.

3   Return value – to pass a single value back from a function.

A function can have any number of parameters, but can only return a single value.

SELF-TEST QUESTION

Given below are the partial specifications of a number of functions. For each function:

1   decide on a name for the function
2   think about how the function would be used
3   decide which items should be parameters
4   decide what (if any) should be returned as the value of the function
5   write the prototype for each function (but do not write the function itself).

The outline descriptions of the functions are:

1   calculate the area of a triangle from a height and base
2   convert a time measured in seconds into hours, minutes and seconds
3   convert a time measured in hours, minutes and seconds into seconds
4   put three characters into alphabetical order
5   given two characters, give the first one (in alphabetical order).

Function main

As we have seen, the function main must appear in every C++ program. It is the first function that is executed when a program starts to run. It is also the last – when main has completed its work, the program ends. It is normal practice to have main appear as the first function at the top of every program.

When your program has stopped, the computer does not stop. When main has finished, control returns to the operating system software. It is possible to tell the operating system whether or not the program was successful by returning either the value 0 (meaning success, nothing went wrong) or the value 1 (meaning failure, the program was not able to complete its task successfully). This is why the function main is declared as having type int:

```
int main (void)
```

In many systems, any value returned by main is ignored by the operating system. In some systems, however, a value does have to be returned. This is normally to say that all was well, so that the function main ends like this:

```
return (0);
}
```

A case study in using functions

We have now discussed all the elements of programming using functions and so we will now see how they can be applied in a small case study. We will trace the development of a small program for a game called rock, scissors, paper, which you may have played as a child (or as an adult).

As played by humans, the game is as follows. Two people face each other, with one hand behind their backs. On a signal, both reveal their hands. A player can make his or her hand signify a rock (clenched fist), a piece of paper (open palm) or a pair of scissors (first and second fingers outstretched). The winner is the person who overcomes the other, according to the following rules. A rock blunts scissors and therefore wins. Scissors cut paper and therefore wins. Paper wraps a rock and therefore wins.

We will construct a program that plays the game. The human player will make a choice – rock, scissors, or paper – but the computer will play randomly. The dialogue between the computer and the player will look like this:

```
Hello
Choose r (for rock), s (for scissors), or p (for paper):
s
You chose scissors.
The computer chose paper
You won!

Another game?
n
Good Bye
```

Now the main part of this program is concerned with deciding whether the person wants to play another game. It looks like this:

```cpp
#include <iostream.h>

int main (void)
{
    char reply;
    void play_game (void);

    cout << "Hello" << endl;
    reply='y';
    while (reply =='y')
        {
        play_game();
        cout << "Another game?" << endl;
```

```
        cin >> reply;
        }
    cout << "Good Bye";
}
```

This main function is small and clear. It deals with one important task – ensuring that further games are played (or not). You can see that main calls just one function, named play_game. The prototype gives us the information that this function has no parameters and does not return a value.

Now we turn our attention to the game itself and write:

```
void play_game (void)
{
        char human_choice, computer_choice;

        void Human_Go (char &);
        void Computer_Go (char &);
        void Decide_who_won (char, char);

        Human_Go (human_choice);
        Computer_Go (computer_choice);
        Decide_who_won (computer_choice, human_choice);
}
```

This function has a header that matches the function prototype – it has no parameters and returns no value. The function uses two pieces of local data – character variables called human_choice and computer_choice. The function consists simply of three function calls, which makes it short and simple. This time, however, the functions have parameters, as indicated by the prototypes and by the function calls.

Let us look at the parameters. The purpose of function Human_Go is to ask the user whether he or she wants to be rock, scissors, or paper. So this function must return some information to play_game. The ampersand alongside the parameter in the prototype indicates precisely that. The same is true of function Computer_Go; it must return a value chosen randomly by the computer. On the other hand, function Decide_who_won needs to be provided with information, but doesn't return any, and so its parameters are merely value parameters.

Function play_game thus illustrates the use of local data, value parameters and reference parameters.

We will now write the function Human_Go:

```
void Human_Go (char & choice)
{
        void display_choice (char);
        cout << "Choose r (for rock), s (for scissors), or p
                (for paper):"
              << endl;
```

```
        cin >> choice;
        cout << "You chose";
        display_choice (choice);
}
```

which inputs the user's choice from the keyboard, displays it and returns the value as the parameter.

Let us now just complete this function display_choice, which translates the single character object into a more descriptive word:

```
void display_choice (char choice)
{
        if (choice == 's') cout << "scissors";
        if (choice == 'r') cout << "rock";
        if (choice == 'p') cout << "paper";
        cout << endl;
}
```

Next the function that makes the computer's choice. For an interesting game, this should be random. The way to do this is to use a random number generator. Such a function is provided as part of one of the C++ libraries. The function rand obtains a random number. If we can obtain a random number which is 0, 1, or 2, we can convert it into a random choice of object (rock, scissors, or paper). The use of this library function is further explained in Appendix C.

A call on rand() provides a random number in the range 0 up to some large integer number. However, we only want a number that is 0, 1, or 2. But the way to get that is to divide the big number by 3 and get the remainder. The % operator does this for us.

```
void Computer_Go (char & choice)
{
        int random_number;
        void display_choice (char);

        random_number=rand() % 3;

        if (random_number==0) choice='r';
        if (random_number==1) choice='s';
        if (random_number==2) choice='p';

        cout << "The computer chose";
        display_choice (choice);
}
```

which returns the random object as the single character parameter.

Because the function uses a library function, we will need an `include` statement at the head of the program:

```
#include <stdlib.h>
```

The remaining function is Decide_who_won, which has all the various tests to carry out:

```
void Decide_who_won (char computer, char human)
{
    if (computer==human)
        cout << "it's a draw!" << endl;
    else
        if ((computer=='p') && (human=='r')
            ||
            (computer=='r') && (human=='s')
            ||
            (computer=='s') && (human=='p'))
            cout << "Computer wins" << endl;
        else
            cout << "You win" << endl;
}
```

The complete program is given in appendix E. It consists of six functions. Each is short, simple and easy to understand – which is ideal. The functions use:

- local data
- value and reference parameters
- a library function.

What this program does not use is a return value. We could have written the function Human_Go as a function that returns a value. As in many programming situations, the choice is a matter of style. Human_Go could be re-written as follows:

```
char Human_Go (void)
{
    void display_choice (char);

    cout << "Choose r (for rock), s (for scissors), or p
            (for paper):"
        << endl;
    cin >> choice;
    cout << "You chose";
    display_choice (choice);
```

```
      return (choice);
}
```

in which case it would be called differently from within the function play_game:

```
human_choice=Human_Go();
```

SELF-TEST QUESTION
Write the prototype for the alternative version of function Human_Go.

SELF-TEST QUESTION
Re-write function Computer.Go so as to use a return value, rather than a parameter.

New language elements

```
return
```

Programming pitfalls

If you write a call to a function which has no parameters, you must have the brackets. So a call to function apple that looks like this:

```
apple;
```

is wrong. It should look like this:

```
apple();
```

Omitting the brackets will not produce compiler error messages. When the program runs it will simply not call the function!

Summary

- One way of passing data back from a function is to return it as the value of the function.
- The value is passed back using the return statement.
- The function header must show the type of the function, or void if the function does not return a value.

Exercises

1 Write a function that returns the product of two floating point numbers. Write the function two ways – using parameters and using a return value.
2 Write a function that finds the largest of its three integer parameters. Your function could make use of function bigger, given above in the text.
3 Write a function that skips anything that is input until either a 'y' or an 'n' is input. The function returns either of these two characters to the calling function.

Games

You now know about the central ingredients of programming and you are ready to tackle bigger programs. Because of their size, these programs need to be constructed from a number of functions.

1 There's a game that elderly people sometimes play to infuriate young children. It's called 'Which Hand'? The elderly person has a sweet hidden in one of his or her hands The person holds out both hands clenched so that the sweet can't be seen. In order to win the sweet, the child has to guess which hand the sweet is in.

 Write a program to simulate the game. The computer randomly chooses which hand the sweet is in (left or right). The player has to guess which hand has the sweet.
2 Pontoon (*vingt-et-un*) is a card game, played by gamblers in casinos. Cards are numbered from 1 to 13 (1 means ace, 11 means jack, 12 means queen, 13 means king). The suit (hearts, diamonds, clubs, spades) of the cards is irrelevant to this game. The player plays against the dealer. The winner is the person whose total score is nearest, but no more than, 21.

 The computer acts as dealer. The computer first deals randomly two cards to the human player. The player can:

 stick, meaning that he or she do not want any more cards
 twist, meaning that he or she would like an additional card
 or is bust, meaning that his or her total has exceeded 21

Once the player has completed his or her business, it is the turn of the dealer.

 Write a program to play the game. Decide on a strategy for the computer to adopt when it is its turn. For example, it could decide to stick if its total is 18 or more.

CHAPTER 10
Global data

Introduction

Global data is the collection of any variables that are declared at the beginning of a program – before the function main. They are accessible to all of the functions in the program.

Local data is the name for the variables that are declared at the start of a particular function. They are accessible only within the function.

Generally, global data is bad; local data is good! We shall see why this is so.

Global data

Global data is declared at the start of a program, after the #include, but before main:

```
#include <iostream.h>

int a, b, c;      // global data
float x, y, z;    // global data


int main (void)
{ etc.
```

Variables that are declared in this position are said to be global to the whole program. They can be accessed from anywhere in the program. This can be useful in special cases, but generally it means that there can be too much indiscriminate access to such variables.

Local data

Local data is the variables that are declared at the top of a function. They provide work space for the function. Consider, for example, a function that outputs a number of asterisks to the screen. It needs a counter to keep track of how many asterisks have been output. This counter is used within the for statement:

```
void display_asterisks()
{
int count;

for (count=0; count <20; count++)
     cout << "*";
}
```

The variable called count has a specific role within the function. There is no reason why it should be used by any other function – and, indeed, it can't! It is separate and local to the function.

Global or local?

Current thinking on programming is very much that global data should be avoided as far as possible. Instead, data should be declared locally and passed as needed to other functions as parameters.

There are occasions, however, where making some data global is the best choice. One example is a program to play the game of chess. It is highly likely that every function within such a program would need access to the data that describes the pieces on the chess board. So, while it would be possible to declare this data locally, it would be very cumbersome – and in such a case the best decision is to make the data global.

A simpler example is, again, a game. Suppose that there is a score that is to be updated at intervals as a game goes on. We will have functions to increase the score, decrease the score and display the score. These functions will be called at the appropriate places within the game program. Declaring the score locally and passing it around the program as a parameter, however worthy, would be long winded and make the program unnecessarily complicated. The best option is to declare it as global.

The best approach to designing the data in a program is to try initially to make it all local. Then, if it seems that this approach will be unwieldy, move selected items of data into the global area.

Later, when you learn about object-oriented programming (outside the scope of this book), you will see how C++ provides other facilities for grouping actions and data in convenient and powerful ways.

Summary

- Global data is declared at the beginning of the program, before the function main.
- Global data is accessible from anywhere in the program.

- Local data is declared at the start of a particular function.
- Local data is accessible only within the function where it is declared.
- Global data should only be used sparingly and occasionally.

Exercise

1 Re-write the following program. Eliminate the global data, replacing it with local data and parameter passing. Retain both the function `main` and the function named swap. The purpose of the program is to input two numbers and to output them in reverse order.

```
#include <iostream.h>

int a, b;
int temp;

int main(void)
{
     void swap (void);

     cin >> a >> b;
     swap();
     cout << a << b;
}

void swap (void)
{
     temp=a;
     a=b;
     b=temp;
}
```

CHAPTER 11

Program design

Introduction

You wouldn't start to design a bridge by thinking about the size of the rivets. You would first make major decisions – like whether the bridge is cantilever or suspension.

You wouldn't begin to design a building by thinking about the colour of the carpets. You would make major decisions first – like how many floors there are to be and where the lifts should be.

Similarly with programming, some people argue that the programmer should start with the major decisions rather than the detail. He or she should do design, do it first and do it well. Decisions about detail – like the positions of semi-colons and brackets – should be postponed. All the stages of programming are crucial, of course, but some are more crucial than others.

This chapter explains how to use one approach to program design. It is called top-down stepwise refinement, or functional decomposition. (These are just overcomplicated terms for a simple method.) The method makes use of a design notation, called pseudo-code.

When you start out to write programs, you usually spend a lot of time in (sometimes tortuous) trial and error. This is often great fun and very creative. Usually you spend some time wrestling with the programming language. It takes some time to learn good practice and to recognize bad practice. It takes even longer to adopt a systematic design approach to programming. The fun remains, the creativity remains, but the nuisance parts of programming are discarded.

Pseudo-code

To free the programmer of the details of the programming language, this design approach employs a design notation called pseudo-code, or program design language (PDL). It uses the following elements:

- sequence
- selection, using **if**
- repetition using **while** and **for**
- functions and function calls.

Here is an example of a design expressed in PDL. The purpose of the program is to find the largest of a series of numbers, input from the keyboard, and terminated by the number −999.

```
function find_largest
  input_number
  largest = number
  while number <> −999
  do
    check_number
    input_number
  endwhile
  display_largest
endfunction

function check_number
  if number > largest
  then
    largest = number
  endif
endfunction
```

You will see that this looks somewhat similar to C++, but that there is very little grammar to worry about. English sentences can be used freely to clarify actions. As in C++, indentation and blank lines are used to aid readability.

As usual, functions are used to avoid any potential complexity – as in the example above.

What this example does not show is the second version of the **if** statement. We can illustrate it with the following example. Suppose we want to input two numbers and to output the larger:

```
function larger
  input two numbers, a and b
  if a > b
    then output a
    else output b
  endif
  endwhile
endfunction
```

The aim of PDL is to provide a useful tool to the programmer, rather than burden him or her with another language.

The main differences between PDL and C++ are:

- every keyword (**if**, **while**, **for**, **function**) has a matching end word

(**endif, endwhile, endfor, endfunction**)
- **while** has the word **do** after the condition
- **if** has the word **then** after the condition
- PDL has no brackets and no semi-colons.

PDL has the following uses:

- it provides an informal notation for exploring alternative designs quickly and easily
- it provides a notation that can be used in conjunction with a design method (functional decomposition in this book)
- it provides a notation for documenting a completed program so that someone else can understand it later.

Functional decomposition

Now that we have looked at a design expressed in PDL – an end-product – we will look at how to carry out design using PDL in conjunction with functional decomposition. We will use the same example.

We begin by writing down a single statement that expresses the overall purpose of the program:

```
find_largest
```

Next we write down, in outline, the necessary steps to accomplish this task:

```
function find_largest
   input_number
   largest = number
   while number <> -999
   do
      check_number
      input_number
   endwhile
   display_largest
endfunction
```

In writing down these steps, we deliberately refrain from going into detail. On the contrary, we try to write down only the main steps that are required. Any detail is described as a function call, to be dealt with later. So the design above describes the main loop in the program without going into detail about how each number is dealt with.

Because PDL is somewhat informal, we can check this design and modify it as necessary without sacrificing a lot of work. For example, the above design is not immediately obvious and we might have to think and explore alternatives before we arrive at it.

The essence of the approach is to concentrate on important matters, postponing attention to detail until later. This is called *top-down design*. The next step is to choose one of the PDL function calls, write it down as a function heading and then write down its constituent steps. For example we could choose the function check_number and design it as follows:

```
check_number
    if number > largest
    then largest = number
    endif
```

The approach continues like this, with each function written down in more and more detail, until we get to the point where the PDL is sufficiently detailed. This is usually when it is obvious what the translation into C++ should be. This process is called *stepwise refinement* or *functional decomposition*.

Case study in design

We now give an outline of how to use the approach in practice. We follow the initial design of a program to play the game of Nim. (You may already have written this program, if you did the exercises at the end of Chapter 4.)

The computer creates three piles of matches, each with a random number of matches in it. The computer then chooses, randomly, who goes first – the computer or the human. Thereafter the two players, the computer and the human, play alternately.

When it is their turn, the players remove as many matches as they like – but at least one, and only from one pile.

The loser is the player who has to take the last match. The winner is the other player.

The computer chooses a pile and a number of matches randomly. The human keys in two numbers – the pile number and the number of matches.

We start with:

```
function Nim
```

and write down the main steps involved:

```
function Nim
  create_three_piles
  decide_who_starts
  while count != zero
  do
```

```
    play
  endwhile
  decide_who_won
endfunction
```

We have expressed the design of the program in terms of a few simple steps. Detail is relegated to function calls. We can check this design to see whether it makes sense. We can also investigate alternative designs. For example, another possible design concerns the alternation of turns. Either player can start and thereafter players take turns. So it is tempting to write the following within the loop, to reflect the alternation:

```
human_plays
computer_plays
```

But this is not going to lead to a satisfactory design, because the game can end whenever either player goes. This is an example of where design is important – we have the chance to get an important ingredient of the design right at an early stage in the development. We can use pseudo-code to explore alternative designs until we are happy with the design. Then we proceed to the next level of detail.

We decide to opt for a variable that describes whose go it is at any point in the game. We will call this variable **player**, and it will have either the value **computer** or the value **human**.

We now embark on what should be one of the easier parts of the design. This is a good approach – to start with the simple things, conquer them and then move on (with renewed confidence) to something more difficult. We choose to design:

```
function decide_who_starts
  get_random_number_zero_or_one
  if number == zero
  then player = human
  else player = computer
  endif
endfunction
```

and then we will design another easy part of the program:

```
function create_three_piles
  pile 1 = random_number_in_range_1_to 32
  pile 2 = random_number_in_range_1_to 32
  pile 3 = random_number_in_range_1_to 32
  count = sum of piles
endfunction
```

Now we address the central function of the top-level design:

```
function play
  if player = human
  then
    human_play
    player = computer
  else
    computer_play
    player = human
  endif
endfunction
```

which deals successfully with the alternation of players. We now have to design two functions – one to play the role of the computer and the other to interact with the human player. The computer first:

```
function computer_play
  randomly_choose_a_non-empty_pile
  obtain_a_random_number_in_the_range_1_to_number_in_pile
  deduct_the_matches_from_the_pile
  update_count
endfunction
```

Here we again see the power of functional decomposition at work. We know that the computer has to choose a pile, but one or more of them may already be empty. We simply postpone thinking about how exactly to do this by making this act into a function call.

The function to elicit the human player's turn might look like this:

```
function human_play
  input_pile_number
  input_number_of_matches
  update_count
endfunction
```

and here we will leave the design, in the interests of preventing the onset of undue detail. In practice, we would have to elaborate some of these functions in more detail, since it is not yet obvious how to design them. An example is the function to choose a random non-empty pile when it is the computer's turn to play.

The advantages of the method

The advantages of using functional decomposition and PDL are:

- top-down design (important things first)
- informality – free of detailed and restricting grammar
- independent of the programming language
- provides documentation.

Design in the real world

Top-down stepwise refinement as described above is just one approach to program design. Other recognized methods are *data structure design* (or the Jackson method), *data flow design* and *object-oriented design*. There are other methods that are not recognized or not regarded as laudable. These include *bottom-up design* and a variety of *ad hoc* methods. The annotated bibliography provides pointers to references on these methods. Perhaps the most important of these approaches for C++ programmers is object-oriented design, since C++ was designed explicitly as an object-oriented language. The book you are reading is about programming using the basics of C++. Books listed in the annotated bibliography go on to tell you about the object-oriented aspects of C++.

Perhaps the most infamous approach to design is called *hacking*. Hacking is not a method at all – it is an anarchic, creative, individual style of programming. The hacker doesn't bother with design at all, but gets straight on the machine, developing the program piece by piece, often in an experimental way (let's see if this works!). Hacking is largely condemned by anyone who purports to be serious in computing. However, it is hard to see how the enthusiastic hobbyist can be prevented from this sort of free expression.

In the world of professional programming, studies of real programmers have been carried out by experimental psychologists to try to find out how they actually carry out program design. (See the references in the annotated bibliography under the heading 'The psychology of programming'.) The results of these studies indicate that real programmers do not use one of the approved design approaches. Instead, they tackle the problem by dividing it (and the program) into parts in an *ad hoc* manner. When the program is complete, they then document the program and create a design document that coincides with one of the approved approaches. So, at the end of the day, it looks as if the program was designed using one of the respectable methods.

Summary

- PDL is a notation for expressing the design of a program.
- PDL has the usual programming structures – **while**, **if**, functions.
- Functional decomposition is one design approach. It uses PDL to develop a design top down, starting with the major elements of the program and successively addressing the more detailed aspects.

- There is a wide variety of approaches to design and evidence that professional programmers use highly personalized methods.
- PDL provides a useful form of documentation for a finished program.

Exercises

Try these fairly small designs to get used to the idea of using PDL.
Design programs to:

1 Input three numbers and display the largest of the numbers.
2 Input a series of numbers, terminated by a negative number. Find the sum of the numbers and the largest of the numbers.
3 Search a one-dimensional array of characters to find a particular character that is input from the keyboard. Display a message to say whether the character was found or not.

Turn to the exercises at the end of every chapter in this book. Select a program specification of interest to you. Design the program using pseudo-code.

Bibliography

There is no book or reference on functional decomposition and pseudo-code. A book that surveys program design methods is:

Program Design by D Bell, I Morrey and J Pugh, Prentice Hall, Hemel Hempstead, forthcoming 1997.

CHAPTER 12
Arrays

Introduction

So far in this book, we have described data items (variables) that are solitary. For example:

```
int count, sum;
char a_char, input_character;
```

These live on their own, performing useful roles in programs as counters, sums, whatever. We can think of these variables as places in memory that have individual names attached to them.

In contrast, we very often in life deal with data that is not discrete, but grouped together into a collection of information. Sometimes the information is in tables. Examples are a train timetable, a pools coupon, a telephone directory. In programming, these things are called data structures. The information in a table is related in some way to other information within the table.

One of the simplest types of data structure in programming is an array. An array can be regarded simply as a table, with a single row of information. This could be either a table of numbers or a table of characters. Here is an array of numbers:

23	54	96	13	7	32

which might represent the ages of a group of people at a party, and here is a table of characters, which holds all the vowels in the English language:

a	e	i	o	u

In C++, a table is called an array. In programming, we refer to an item in an array by its position in the array. To us humans, the character a is in the first position in this table, but in C++ the first position in an array is called the zeroth position. Successive positions in an array are the zeroth, first, second, third, etc. Thus the character o is in the third position in the above array. In programming, the position of an item in an array is called the subscript (or sometimes an index). We can therefore picture an array, together with its subscripts, like this:

array:	a	e	i	o	u

subscripts: 0   1   2   3   4

Remember that the subscripts aren't held in computer memory – only the data.

Here is another array, this time containing numbers. The subscripts for the array are also shown:

array:	34	78	54	12	21	35

subscripts: 0   1   2   3   4   5

Declaring an array

In C++, an array is declared just like any other variable, either at the top of the program (before function main) or at the top of a particular function. The programmer gives the array a name, like this:

```
int ages[6];
char vowels[5];
```

As with any other variable, it is usual (and a good idea) to choose a name for the array that describes clearly what it is going to be used for. The name is the name for the complete array – the complete collection of data. When you declare an array, you say how long it is, that is how many items it is going to contain.

The array called ages is big enough to contain six numbers, with subscripts going from 0 to 5. The array called vowels is big enough to contain five characters. The subscripts go from 0 to 4.

The rules for choosing the name of an array are the same as for choosing any other name (data or function) in C++. See Appendix D.

SELF-TEST QUESTION
Declare an array to hold figures for the rain that falls each day for a week.

Subscripts

The way that the program refers to an individual item in an array is to specify a subscript value. Thus age[3] refers to the element in the array with subscript 3 – the value 12 in this case. Similarly, vowels [2] contains the letter i.

We can input a value for an element of an array like this:

```
cin >> ages[2];
cin >> vowels[3];
```

and similarly output values:

```
cout << ages[0] << ages[2];
cout << vowels[3];
```

We can change the values with assignment statements, like this:

```
ages[3] = 99;
vowels[2] = 'x';
```

In all these program fragments, we are referring to individual elements in an array by specifying the value of a subscript that identifies the particular element that we are interested in.

SELF-TEST QUESTION
Given the declaration:

```
int table[2];
```

how long is the array and what is the valid range of subscripts?

Very often, we want to refer to the nth element in an array, where n is a variable. This is how the power of arrays really comes into its own. Suppose, for example, we want to add up all the numbers in an array (of numbers). Let's suppose that we have an array with seven elements that hold the number of computers sold in a shop during each day in a week:

```
int sale[7];
```

The clumsy way to add up the sales would be to write:

```
sum=sale[0]+sale[1]+sale[2]+sale[3]+sale[4]+sale[5]+
   sale[6];
```

which is quite correct, but does not exploit the regularity of an array. The alternative would be to use a `for` loop. A variable is used to hold the value of the subscript representing the day of the week. The subscript is made initially equal to 0 and then incremented each time the loop is repeated:

```
int sale[7], sum;
int day;
```

```
sum=0;
for (day=0; day<7; day++)
{
    sum=sum+sale[day];
}
```

This program fragment is no shorter than what it replaces. But it would be if the array had 1000 items to add up!

Subscripts are the one place in programming when it is permissible (sometimes) to use a name that is a little cryptic. In the above program fragment, however, using the name day as the subscript is clear and relates strongly to the problem being solved.

SELF-TEST QUESTION
What would this do?

```
int sale[7], sum;
int day;

sum=0;
for (day=0; day<=7; day++)
{
    sum=sum+sale[day];
}
```

Passing arrays as parameters

As we have seen in earlier chapters of this book, functions are very important in programming. Part of using functions is passing information to and from functions as parameters. This is how to pass arrays as parameters.

Suppose we want to write a function whose job it is to calculate the sum of the elements in an array of integers. Being perceptive programmers, we want the function to be general purpose, that is able to deal with arrays of any length. So the parameters to be passed to the function are:

the array
the length of the array

and the parameter (or result) to be returned to the user of the function is a number, the sum of the values.

The prototype is:

```
void sum(int array[], int length, int & total)
```

A call on the function looks like this:

```
int table[24];

sum (table, 24, result);
```

The function itself is:

```
void sum(int array[], int length, int & total)
{
    int s;

    total = 0;
    for(s=0; s<length; s++)
        total = total+array[s];
}
```

Notice that in the header for the function, the array is declared as usual with square brackets, but with nothing inside the square brackets. This is to specify that the parameter is an array, but without spelling out how long the array actually is. Because it will accept an array of any length, this function is general purpose and potentially very useful. This is highly preferable to a special-purpose function that will only work when the array is, say, eight elements long.

The name used for the subscript in this function is simply s. This is an example of where the name that has been chosen is cryptic. Because the function is general purpose, we do not know the purpose of the array or the meaning of the subscript.

SELF-TEST QUESTION
Write a function that displays an array of characters on the screen. The parameters of the function are the array and its length.

In the above example, the function merely uses the array, without changing its value. As we have seen, when a parameter to a function does get changed by the function, it has to be flagged in the function header with an ampersand (&). This is the case with the parameter total.

Now we look at an example where the function does change the array. Suppose we want a function to fill an array with zeros; this obviously involves changing the array. The prototype is:

```
void fill_zero (int array[], int length);
```

A call on the function would typically be:

```
int table[8];
fill_zero (table, 8);
```

and the function itself is:

```
void fill_zero (int array[], int length)
{
      for(s=0;  s<8;  s++)
          array[s] = 0;
}
```

in which, as you will have noticed, the array parameter, although it is to be changed by the function, does not have an & in front of it. You will remember that the normal rule is that any parameter that is going to be changed by a function must have an & before its name in the function header (and in the prototype). But now we have an exception to the general rule.

The rule is:

When an array is used as a parameter to a function, it never needs an & in front of it, even if its value is changed by the function.

The reason for what is an exception to the general rule lies in the detail of the way in which parameter passing is implemented. This detail need not concern us.

SELF-TEST QUESTION
Write a function that inputs the values of an array of integers. The parameters for the function are the array and its length.

Common operations on arrays

In this section we look at a number of useful things that are commonly done with arrays.

A common sequence of things that are done with arrays is:

1   input some values for the elements of the array
2   carry out some action on the array (for illustration, multiply each of the elements of the array by itself)
3   output the values in the array.

We will now look at each of these in turn.
Given an array:

```
int table[10];
```

we can input some values from the keyboard and place the values in the array like this:

```
for (i=0; i<10; i++)
    cin >> table[i];
```

Now to multiply each of the elements of the array by itself:

```
for (i=0; i<10; i++)
    table[i] = table[i]*table[i];
```

Finally, we can output the values of the array like this:

```
for (i=0; i<10; i++)
    cout << table[i];
```

You will see that it is very common to see the for statement used in conjunction with arrays. In fact, for loops are often used to process arrays. They go together like a horse and carriage, love and marriage. It is, of course, because a for loop makes the maximum use of the uniformity of arrays.

Another illustrative action that can be performed on an array is finding the largest value. One approach is to start by assuming that the first item is the largest. Then we look at each element in turn, comparing it with this largest value. If we find a value that is larger than the one we have already got, we update our largest value.

```
int table[10];
int largest, i;

largest = table[0];

for (i=0; i<10; i++)
    if (table[i] > largest) largest = table[i];
```

SELF-TEST QUESTION
Alter the piece of program to find the largest item in an array so that it also finds the position (subscript number) of the largest element.

Arrays are of fixed length

Once you have declared an array like this:

```
int table[10];
```

you cannot change it. Arrays are not made of elastic; they are made of quick-setting concrete.

Suppose we want to write a piece of program to input someone's name and store it in an array. Let us suppose that a name ends with a full stop like this:

Janet.

The program fragment to input a name is given below. Notice that the loop uses a while rather than the for. This is because we do not know in advance how long a name is going to be. Instead we have to continue inputting until the full stop is reached.

```
char name[20];
int s;
char c;

cin >> c;
s=0;
while (c != '.')
        {
        name[s]=c;
        cin >> c;
        s++;
        }
```

Now people's names are, of course, different in size – some are long and some are short. As programmers, we have to choose a definite, fixed size for any array that we use. The only strategy that we can adopt is to make the array long enough to cope with any name. The trouble is that whatever length we choose (say 20 characters as in the program fragment above), it is always possible that someone will have a name that is even longer. Unless we build some protection into the program, it will blindly input characters and store them in computer memory beyond the end of the array. The computer will issue no error message, either at compile time or when the program is running. A change will have been made to some unknown piece of data – and this is sure to have some undesirable repercussions later on.

This piece of program can be made more robust if a check is made to see whether the end of the array has been reached:

```
char name[20];
int s;
char c;

cin >> c;
s=0;
while ((c != '.') && (s<20))
        {
```

```
name[s]=c;
cin >> c;
s++;
}
```

Now the loop ends either when the full stop is encountered or when the end of the array is reached.

We have seen that an array has a definite, fixed size, and we have seen one way of coping with this. More advanced features of C++, like pointers and linked lists (beyond the scope of this book), provide greater flexibility.

SELF-TEST QUESTION
In the above program fragment, the condition in the while loop is quite complicated. Can it be written differently? Does the following condition perform the same task?

```
while ( !((c='.') || (s=20)) )
```

Using const

In a program with several arrays, there are the declarations of the arrays and almost certainly lots of for loops. The arrays, together with their lengths, will be passed around the program as parameters. There is plenty of scope for confusion, particularly if two different arrays have the same length.

Suppose, for example, we are writing a program to analyze marks that students obtain in assignments. Suppose there are 10 students. We want one array to hold the average mark for each student:

```
int student_mark[10];
```

By coincidence, there are also 10 courses. We also want a second array to hold the average mark for each course:

```
int course_mark[10];
```

The problem is that, wherever we see the number 10 in the program, we do not know whether it is the number of students or the number of courses. As things stand, of course, it doesn't matter – because they are the same! But suppose we needed to alter the program so that it deals with 20 students. We would very much like to change every occurrence of the number 9 by the number 19 using a handy text editor. But because the arrays are the same length, this would cause great damage to the program.

One way to clarify such a program is to declare the lengths of the arrays as constants, like this:

```
const int students = 10;
int student_mark[students];

const int courses = 10;
int course_mark[courses];
```

and now we can make changes to the program with supreme confidence, simply by changing one number in the constant declaration.

SELF-TEST QUESTION
A program is to store and manipulate rainfall figures for each day of the week. An array is to be used to store the seven values. Write C++ statements to declare the array and to fill it with zeros. Make use of `const` as appropriate.

Initializing an array

Initializing means giving a variable an initial or starting value. If you write this:

```
int table[10];
```

then an array is set up in memory and the array contains junk. What is in the array is whatever was in that place in memory when the memory was last used. Whatever it was, it certainly won't be useful information. There is a common misconception that an array is automatically set up with zeros in all its elements (if it is an array of numbers). This is not true.

One way to initialize an array is to use a loop, like this:

```
for (i=0; i<10; i++)
    table[i] = 0;
```

Another way of initializing an array is to declare it like this:

```
int table[10] = {0};
```

which is now another use for the curly brackets. This initializes the complete array – every element – to the value 0. The initialization is carried out once, when the array is created. If the program changes the value of an element in the array, the value will not change back to its original value – not until the program is run again.

If the program needs periodically to reset the array back to its initial values, then the way to do it is by using the `for` loop as shown above.

SELF-TEST QUESTION
Declare an array of 100 characters and fill it with the letter x as part of the declaration.

Programming pitfalls

A common error in C++ is to confuse the length of an array with the range of valid subscripts. For example, the array:

```
int table[10];
```

has 10 elements. The valid range of subscripts for this array is 0 to 9. Reference to table[10] will give rise to weird and wonderful effects, which will generally be undesirable. Unfortunately, no error checking is carried out, either when the program is compiled or when the program is running.

Here is a common example of how to do things wrongly:

```
int table[10]; int s;

for (s=0; s <= 10; s++)
    table[s] = 0;
```

This will place a zero in all of the elements of the array table, but then go on to place a zero in whatever data item happens to be immediately after the array in computer memory. If this is your bank balance, this may or may not be a problem, depending on your financial circumstances!

Summary

- An array is a collection of data. It is given a name by the programmer.
- An array is declared, along with other variables, like this:
  ```
  int harry[24];
  ```
  in which 24 is the length of the array (the number of items it will contain).
- An individual element in an array is referred to by an integer subscript, for example:
  ```
  harry[12] = 45;
  ```
- It is common to use the for loop in conjunction with arrays.
- In parameter passing, an array never needs an & in the function header or in the prototype.

Exercises

Basic operations on arrays

1 Write a program that uses an array of 10 numbers. Then write functions that carry out each of the following operations.

Input values from the keyboard for the values of all of the elements of the array.
Output all the values. (You can now check that they have been entered correctly into your array.)
Add up the values and display the total.
Find the largest value and the smallest value.
Input a value from the keyboard and search to see whether it is present in the array. Display a message to say whether it is present in the array or not.

2 Write a program that uses an array of 10 characters. Then write functions that carry out each of the following operations.

Input values from the keyboard for the values of all of the elements of the array.
Output all the values. (You can now check that they have been entered correctly into your array.)
Input a value from the keyboard and search to see whether it is present in the array. Display a message to say whether it is present in the array or not.

If you have done all of these successfully, then arrays should hold no mysteries for you!

Statistics

Write a program that inputs a series of numerical data values into an array. The numbers are in the range 0 to 100. The numbers are terminated with some special value – say a negative number.
  Calculate:

the largest number
the smallest number
the sum of the numbers
the mean of the numbers.

Display a histogram that shows how many numbers are in the ranges 0 to 9, 10 to 19, etc., like this:

0 to 9: *

```
10 to 19:  ****
10 to 19:  *******
10 to 19:  *****
```

Random numbers

Check to see that the random number generator function is working correctly. Set it up to provide random numbers in the range 1 to 100. Then call the function 100 times, placing the frequencies in an array as in the last exercise. Finally display the frequency histogram, again as in the last exercise.

Words

1 Write a program that inputs a word from the keyboard and then displays all possible combinations and permutations of the word. So, for example, if the word 'cat' is entered, then the following are output:

cat, atc, act, tac, tca, ca, ac, ta, at, ta, at, c, a, t

2 A palindrome is a word that is spelled the same backwards as forwards. So, for example, the word 'madam' is a palindrome, but the word 'bolton' is not. Write a program that inputs a word and tests to see if it is a palindrome.

Information processing – searching

1 Set up an array to contain the vowels in the English language. Then input any character from the keyboard and check whether it is a vowel (that is, whether it is in the array or not).
2 Set up an array to contain the winning six numbers in a lottery. Then input six numbers one by one, and check whether they are in the array or not.
3 Each member of a library has a unique user code, an integer. When someone wants to borrow a book, a check is made that the user code is valid. Write a program that searches a table of user codes to find a particular code. The program should display a message saying that the code is either valid or invalid.

Information processing – sorting

1 Write a program that inputs a series of numbers, sorts them into ascending numerical order and then displays the numbers.
This program is not the easiest to write. There are very many approaches to sorting – in fact there are whole books on the subject! One approach is as follows.
Find the smallest number in the array. Swap it with the first item in the

array. Now the first item in the array is in the right place. Leave this first item alone and repeat the operation on the remainder of the array (everything except the first item). Repeat, carrying out this operation on a smaller and smaller array until the complete array is in order.

CHAPTER 13

Arrays – two dimensional

Introduction

Two-dimensional arrays, or tables, are very common in everyday life:

a chess board
a train timetable
a lottery ticket
a spreadsheet.

In the previous chapter, we looked at one-dimensional arrays. C++ provides a natural extension of one-dimensional arrays to two dimensions. So, for example, the declaration:

```
int table[3][5];
```

declares a two-dimensional array of integers. The array is called table. We can think of it as having three rows and five columns. We can picture it like this:

22	49	4	93	32
3	8	67	51	63
54	0	76	31	99

Declaring an array

An array is declared just like any other variables, either at the top of the program or at the top of a particular function. The programmer gives the array a name, like this:

```
int sales[5][6];
char chess_board[8][8];
```

As with any other variable, it is usual (and a good idea) to choose a name for the array that describes clearly what it is going to be used for. The name is the name for the complete array – the complete collection of data. The rules for choosing the name of an array are the same as for choosing any other name (data or function) in C++. See Appendix´D.

When you declare an array, you say how many columns and how many rows it has.

The array called sales has five rows – one for each of five salespeople. It has six columns – one for each working day in the week. The array contains sales figures for each of five people for each day of the week.

```
int sales[5][6].
```

We might also set up an array, called temps, to hold information about the temperatures in each of 10 ovens, each hour during a 24 hour period:

```
float temps[10][24];
```

SELF-TEST QUESTION
Declare an array to represent a chess board. A chess board is eight squares by eight squares. Each position in the array should hold a single character.

Subscripts

With a two-dimensional array, the way that the program refers to an individual item is to specify the values of two subscripts. Thus sales[3][2] refers to the element in the array with row 3 and column 2 – salesperson number 3 and the day Thursday. Similarly, chess_board[2][8] might contain the letter p (for pawn).

We can input a value for an element of an array like this:

```
cin >> sales[2][3];
cin >> chess_board[3][4]; // place a piece on a square
```

and similarly output values:

```
cout << sales[0][1] << sales[2][1];
cout << chess_board[3][8];
```

We can change the values with assignment statements, like this:

```
sales[3][2] = 99;
chess_board[2][7] = 'k'; // place a knight on a square
```

In all these program fragments, we are referring to individual elements in an array by specifying the values of the subscripts that identify the particular element that we are interested in.

Very often, we want to refer to an element in an array by specifying *variables* for each of the two subscripts. This is the way in which the power of arrays really comes into its own.

Suppose, for example, we want to add up all the numbers in an array of numbers. An array holds data on sales of computers in five shops over a period of seven days. The array has five rows, each holding the number of computers sold in one of five shops. The array has seven columns, one for each day in a week. So the array holds the sales figures for each shop, for each day of the week:

```
int sale[5][7];
```

The clumsy way to add up the sales would be to write:

```
sum=sale[0][0]+sale[0][1]+sale[0][2]+sale[0][3]+sale[0][4]
   +sale[0][5]+sale[0][6]+sale[1][0]+sale[1][1]+sale[1][2]
   +sale[1][3]+sale[1][4]+sale[1][5]+sale[1][6] + ...
```

which is long winded, but quite correct. However, it does not exploit the regularity of an array. The alternative would be to use a for loop. Variables are used to hold the values of the subscripts. Each subscript is made initially equal to 0 and then incremented each time the loop is repeated:

```
int sale[5][7], sum;
int shop, day;

sum=0;
for (shop=0; shop<5; shop++)
      for (day=0; day<7; day++)
            sum=sum+sale[shop][day];
```

which is considerably shorter and much neater than if we had written out all the sums in explicit detail.

SELF-TEST QUESTION
Write C++ statements to place a space character on every square of an 8 by 8 chess board that is represented as a two-dimensional array of characters.

Passing arrays as parameters

Functions are a vital ingredient in programming and a major facet of using functions is passing information to and from functions as parameters. We now look at how to pass two-dimensional arrays as parameters.

Suppose we want to write a function whose job it is to calculate the sum of the elements in an array of integers. Being perceptive programmers, we want the function to be general purpose, that is able to deal with arrays of any length. So the parameters to be passed to the function are:

the array
the number of columns in the array
the number of rows in the array.

and the parameter (or result) to be returned to the user of the function is a number, the sum of the values.

This is one of the few places in C++ where the beauty of the language breaks down a little – as we shall see in a moment.

The prototype looks like this:

```
void sum(int array[][12], int rows, int & total);
```

which means that the array that the function uses must have 12 columns. However, the number of rows is a variable, passed as a parameter.

The snag with passing two-dimensional arrays as parameters is that the number of columns (the second of the two dimensions) must be explicitly declared in the definition of the function. This unfortunately means that such functions are much less flexible than they might be. (The explanation for this restriction lies deep in the mechanism by which parameters are passed in C++ and we will not explore the detail here.) Thankfully, the first dimension, the number of rows, can be a variable parameter.

A call on the function looks like this:

```
int table[24][12];

sum (table, 24, result);
```

The function itself is:

```
void sum(int array[][12], int rows, int & total)
{
      int row, col;

      total = 0;
      for (row=0; row < rows; row++)
            for (col=0; col < 12; col++)
                  total = total+array[row][col];
}
```

In the above example, the function merely *uses* the array, without *changing* its value. As we have seen, when a parameter to a function does get changed by the function, it has to be flagged in the function header with an ampersand (&). This is the case with the parameter total.

Now we look at an example where the function does change the array. Suppose we want a function to fill an array with zeros; this obviously involves changing the array. A call on the function would typically be:

```
int table[5][8];

fill_zero (table[][8], 5);
```

and the function itself is:

```
int fill_zero (array[][8], int length)
{
    int row, col;
    for(row=0; row<length; row++)
        for(col=0; col<8; col++)
            array[row][col]= 0;
}
```

in which, as you will have noticed, the array parameter, although it is to be changed by the function, does not have an & in front of it.

As with one-dimensional arrays, the rule is:

When an array is used as a parameter to a function, it never needs an & in front of it, even if its value is changed by the function.

SELF-TEST QUESTION
Write a C++ function to place a space character on every square of an 8 by 8 chess board that is represented as a two-dimensional array of characters. Try to make the function as general as possible. For example, the name of the array should ideally be a parameter. Is it possible to make the size of the array, that is the number of rows and columns, a parameter?

Common operations on arrays

In this section we look at a number of useful things that are commonly done with arrays.

A common sequence of things that are done with arrays is:

1 input some values for the elements of the array

2   carry out some action on the array (for illustration, multiply each of the elements of the array by itself)
3   output the values in the array.

We will now look at each of these in turn.
    Given an array:

```
int table[10][5];
```

we can input some values from the keyboard and place the values in the array like this:

```
int row, col;

for (row=0; row<10; row++)
    for (col=0; col<5; col++)
        cin >> table[row][col];
```

Now to multiply each of the elements of the array by itself:

```
for (row=0; row<10; row++)
    for (col=0; col<5; col++)
        table[row][col] =
table[row][col]*table[row][col];
```

Finally, we can output the values of the array like this:

```
for (row=0; row<10; row++)
    for (col=0; col<5; col++)
        cout << table[row][col];
```

You will see again that it is very common to see the `for` statement used in conjunction with arrays. In fact, in most programs where arrays are used, the `for` statement is used to process them. The reason is that a `for` loop makes the maximum use of the uniformity of arrays.

SELF-TEST QUESTION
Re-write the above sample operations on arrays (input values, output the values, multiply each element by itself) as functions that are as general purpose as possible.

Using `const`

In a program with several arrays, there are the declarations of the arrays and almost certainly lots of `for` loops. The arrays, together with their lengths, will be passed around the program as parameters. There is plenty of scope for confusion, particularly if two different arrays have the same length.

For example, in a program to analyze the sales figures of computers at a number of shops over a number of days, we need a two-dimensional array to hold the figures. Each column represents a day. The rows are the data for each shop. Now suppose that, by coincidence, there are seven shops. The array is:

```
int sale[7][7];
```

The problem is that, wherever we see the number 7 in the program, we do not know whether it is the number of shops or the number of days. As things stand, of course, it doesn't matter – because they are the same! But suppose we needed to alter the program so that it deals with eight shops. We would very much like to change every occurrence of the number 7 to the number 8 using a handy text editor. This is impossibly dangerous because the lengths are the same.

An excellent way to clarify such a program is to declare the lengths as constants, like this:

```
const int days = 7;
const int shops = 7;
```

and then the array as:

```
int sale[shops][days];
```

Now that we have the constant declarations, a for loop looks like this:

```
for (s = 0; s < shops; s++)
```

and now we can make changes to the program with confidence, simply by changing one number in the constant declaration.

Initializing an array

Initializing means giving a variable an initial or starting value. If you write this:

```
int table[10][10];
```

then an array is set up in memory and the array contains junk. What is in the array is whatever was in that place in memory when the memory was last used. Whatever it was, it certainly won't be useful information. There is a common misconception that an array of numbers is automatically set up with zeros in all its elements. *This is not true.*

One way to initialize an array is to use nested loops, like this:

```
for (row=0; row<10; row++)
    for (col=0; col<10; col++)
        table[row][col] = 0;
```

Another way of initializing an array is to declare it like this:

```
int table[10][10] = {0};
```

which is now another use for the curly brackets. This initializes the complete array – every element – to the value 0. The initialization is carried out once, when the array is created. If the program changes the value of an element in the array, the value will not change back to its original value – not until the program is run again.

If the program needs periodically to reset the array back to its initial values, then the way to do it is with the for loops as shown above.

SELF-TEST QUESTION
Write the declaration of a 10 by 10 array of characters in such a way that the array is filled with spaces.

Programming pitfalls

A common error in C++ is to confuse the length of an array with the range of valid subscripts.

For example, the array:

```
int table[10][10];
```

has 10 rows and 10 columns. The valid range of subscripts (for the rows and for the columns) is 0 to 9. Reference to table[10][10] will give rise to weird and wonderful effects, which will generally be undesirable.

Summary

- A two-dimensional array is a collection of data in a table, with rows and columns.
- An array is given a name by the programmer.
- An array is declared, along with other variables, like this:

```
int Alice[24][23];
```

in which 24 is the number of rows in the array and 23 is the number of columns.

- An individual element of an array is referred to by an integer subscript, for example:

    ```
    Alice[12][3] = 45;
    ```

- There is a restriction on passing the array dimensions as parameters to a function.
- It is common to use the for loop in conjunction with arrays.

Exercises

Basic operations on two-dimensional arrays

1 Write a program that uses a 5 by 6 array of numbers. Then write functions that carry out each of the following operations.

   Input values from the keyboard for the values of all of the elements of the array.
   Output all the values. (You can now check that they have been entered correctly into your array.)
   Add up the values for each of the six columns and display them.
   Add up all the values of each of the five rows and display them.
   Find the largest value in the first row and the smallest value in the last column.
   Find the largest value in the complete array.
   Input a value from the keyboard and search to see whether it is present in the array. Display a message to say whether it is present in the array or not.

If you have done all of these successfully, then two-dimensional arrays should hold no mysteries for you!

2 The transpose of an array is the technical term used to describe swapping the elements in an array across one of the diagonals. The numbers on the diagonal do not change. So if an array was:

```
 1    2    3    4
 6    7    8    9
10   11   12   13
14   15   16   17
```

then its transpose is:

```
1    6   10   14
2    7   11   15
3    8   12   16
4    9   13   17
```

Write a program that inputs the elements of an array, transposes it and outputs it.

Information processing – searching and lookup

1 Set up a two-dimensional array that holds the names of a number of people, like this:

a	l	i	c	e	*
t	o	m	*		
p	e	t	e	r	*
m	i	k	e	*	
s	u	s	a	n	*

Each row ends with an asterisk to signify the end of the name.

A second, one-dimensional array holds the age of each of the people. One row of the array that holds names corresponds to one row of the array that holds ages.

Write a program that inputs a name from the keyboard and searches for the name in the array. Then display the age of that person.

Games

1 Noughts and crosses is played on a 3 by 3 grid, which is initially blank. Each of two players goes in turn. One places a cross in a blank square; the other places a nought in a blank square.

The winner is the person who gets a line of three noughts or three crosses. Thus a win for noughts might look like this:

```
0   x   0
x   0
x       0
```

Write a program to play the game. One player is the computer, which decides where to play on a random basis.

2 Battleships is a game normally played by two people using paper and pencil. In this version, a person plays the computer. The computer also records and displays the status of the game. When it is the computer's turn to play, it always plays completely randomly. The game is also slightly simplified.

Each of the two players has two 10 by 10 grids. One is called the home fleet and the other is called the enemy fleet. Each player keeps these grids secret from the other player.

Initially, both players place 10 battleships somewhere on their home grid. The computer places its ships randomly, but the human can, of course, play with a strategy. Places on the grid are specified by a row number and a column number, in the range 1 to 10. An example home grid is:

	b		b						
				b					
	b								
			b			b			
		b			b	b			
			b						

The computer determines randomly who goes first. Players then play in turn.

A player 'fires' a shot, by specifying a row number and column number. The player marks this position on his or her own enemy grid, to remember where shots have been fired. The opponent honestly declares whether a ship has been sunk or not, and marks the position of the shot on his or her own home grid.

Play continues until all the ships of one player have been sunk. This player loses and the opponent wins.

Artificial life

An organism consists of single cells that are on (alive) or off (dead). Each generation of life consists of a single row of cells. Each generation of life (each row) of the organism depends on the previous one (just like real life). Time moves downwards, from top to bottom. Each row represents a generation. The lives look like this:

					*					
				*	*	*				
			*	*		*	*			
		*	*		*	*	*	*		
	*	*			*				*	
*	*		*	*	*	*		*	*	*

or, without the encompassing array lines:

```
                        *
                  *   *   *
               *   *           *
            *   *       *   *   *   *
         *   *           *               *
      *   *       *   *   *   *       *   *   *
```

In the beginning, there is just one cell alive. Whether a cell is alive or dead depends on a combination of factors: whether or not it was alive in the last generation and whether or not its immediate neighbours were alive in the last generation. You can see that, even after only five generations, a pattern is emerging. The rules are as follows.

A cell lives only if:

it was dead, but only its left neighbour was alive
it was dead, but only its right neighbour was alive
it was alive, but its immediate neighbours were dead
it was alive, and only its right neighbour was alive

So, for example, given the following generation:

```
 _____
|   | * | * | * |   |
 _____
```

The first cell lives, because even though it was dead, its immediate right neighbour was alive.
The second cell lives because only its immediate right neighbour was alive.
The third living cell dies (through overcrowding, we surmise!).
The fourth cell dies.
The fifth cell lives because, although it was dead, its immediate left neighbour was alive.

So the new generation is:

```
 _____
| * | * |   |   | * |
 _____
```

Write a program that uses a two-dimensional array to chart the progress of the life form. Display the development on the screen as asterisks, as above.

2 *Conway's Game of Life.* In this life form, again, an organism consists of single cells that are on (alive) or off (dead). In this form of life, the organisms exist in a two-dimensional grid world, for example:

		*		*			
	*		*	*			
			*		*		
		*					
	*						

The rules governing this organism are:

1 If a live cell has two or three neighbours, it will survive. Otherwise it will die of isolation or overcrowding.
2 If an empty cell is surrounded by exactly three cells, then a new live cell will be 'born' to fill the space.
3 All 'births' and 'deaths' take place simultaneously.

Write a program to simulate this kind of life. The program should initially input a set of co-ordinates (row and column numbers) for each cell that is alive.

The program needs two arrays – one to represent the current state of life and another to represent the next generation. After a new generation is created, the roles of the two arrays are swapped.

CHAPTER 14

Pointers

Introduction

The idea of a pointer is sophisticated. Novice readers should, perhaps, skip this chapter until they are confident. Pointers play a large role in the language C. But one of the strengths of C++ is that this fairly complex facility has a much smaller role. Therefore, in this book, the treatment of pointers is confined to this chapter and the chapter on strings.

The concept of a pointer

Let us start by reviewing the idea of a variable. The concept of a variable is central to programming. This book introduced early the idea of a variable and has used it extensively thereafter. A variable is a named item that contains a value. The value can change as the program executes. In C++ a variable is declared like this:

```
int Ben;
```

which creates a single variable called Ben which is able to hold a single integer. The variable does not have a defined value until we give it one. One way to do this is by using an assignment:

```
Ben = 45;
```

We can think of a variable like Ben as a labelled box in memory with a value inside it:

Ben | 45 |

A pointer is a variable that points to some other variable. We can declare a pointer like this:

```
int * x;
```

The * means that this variable is not an integer, but a pointer. The int means that this pointer will point to integer variables and not to other types, like floating point

118

and character variables. The name of this pointer is x; as usual, we can give a pointer variable a name of our choosing. As declared, this variable is ready and willing to receive a pointer, but as yet has no defined value.

The 'pointer to' operator

We can give a pointer variable a value using an assignment statement like this:

```
int *x;

x = &Ben;
```

The & operator means 'pointer to'. So the complete statement reads 'the variable x becomes equal to a pointer to the variable Ben'.

We can now picture these variables like this:

Ben   45

x

We can use any number of pointer variables, and choose to make them point to the same place:

```
int Ben;

int *x, *p;

Ben = 78;
x = &Ben;
p = &Ben;
```

SELF-TEST QUESTION
Draw a diagram to illustrate what has happened to Ben, x and p.

The 'item pointed to by' operator

There is one final step in the story about pointers. To illustrate it, we will declare two integer variables and a pointer variable:

```
int Bill, Ben;

int *p;
```

As before, we will give Bill a value and make p point to Bill:

```
Bill = 63;
p = &Bill;
```

Now suppose that we want to copy the value in Bill into the variable Ben. The obvious way to do this is:

```
Ben = Bill;
```

But there is another way, using the pointer. In the variable p we have a pointer to Bill. We can use the pointer to obtain the value:

```
Ben = *p;
```

The operator * means 'item pointed to by'. So this statement reads 'Ben becomes equal to the item pointed to by p'. Now we know that p points to Bill, so Ben becomes equal to Bill.

You will see that the asterisk operator is used in two different places, with two different meanings. We used it in an assignment statement to obtain the item pointed to by a pointer. It is also used when we declare a pointer variable, as in:

```
int * x;
```

to mean that x is a pointer to an integer.

SELF-TEST QUESTION
Work out what this program extract does:

```
int i, j;
int * p1, * p2;

i = 66;
p1 = &i;
p2 = p1;
j = *p2;
```

Using pointers

We can improve our understanding of programs with pointers if we look at some pieces of program, including pieces that have some errors in them.

We will declare an integer variable and a pointer:

```
int i;
int * p;
```

Now we give the integer a value:

```
i = 99;
```

which is straightforward. But what if we now do this?

```
p = i;
```

This is erroneous. The variable p is designed to hold a pointer. But we are trying to give it a value that is an integer.

How about doing this?

```
p = 77;
```

This again is erroneous, for the same reason.

Finally, how about this?

```
p = & i;
```

This, at last, is OK.

You will see that programming with pointers is exacting – statements that look innocent are often faulty.

We have seen how to declare and use pointers. Programs that use pointers are decorated with & and *. Such programs can seem to be very cryptic. These small operators pack a lot of meaning. Writing and reading a program that uses pointers demands high concentration. Drawing diagrams that show the variables and pointers is often useful.

How pointers are implemented

An understanding of pointers can be enhanced by an understanding of how they work. This requires an understanding of memory addresses. If you are not totally happy about your understanding of addresses, you might be best advised to skip this section.

Variables are allocated space in the main memory of the computer by the C++ compiler and linker. The memory of a computer consists of thousands or millions of bytes of information. The bytes are numbered from zero upwards, so that each byte is uniquely identified. This identification is known as the address of the byte of information. The instructions in a program make use of the addresses in order to refer to the data items in memory. A pointer variable is simply a variable that contains the address of another place in memory – the address of another variable.

The following diagram illustrates this idea. It shows computer memory, with each byte having its own address. It shows an integer variable called Jane, which has the value 46. It also shows another variable, Anne, which contains a pointer to Jane – the address of Jane.

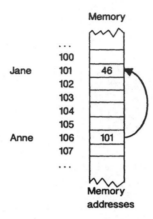

Pointers and parameters

Pointers are actually employed in parameter passing. This has not been mentioned until now because it is easy to use parameters without knowing anything about pointers. You do not need to know about pointers to use parameters in C++.

You will recall that if a parameter is passed by value, it can be used by the function but not changed. This is termed *call by value*, and such parameters are called *value parameters*.

As an example, here is a function call:

```
int number;
output_please (number);
```

and here is the function itself:

```
void output_please (int x)
{
cout << x;
}
```

This is actually implemented by passing a copy of the value of the parameter for use by the function. Thus, even if the function does try to change the value, the original value is preserved intact.

The other kind of parameter is one that can be used and changed by the function. This is termed *call by reference* and such parameters are termed *reference parameters*. A parameter of this type must be specially marked by an ampersand in the function header and prototype. As an example, here is a function call:

```
int number;
input_please (number);
```

and here is the function itself:

```
void input_please (int & x)
{
cin >> x;
}
```

The ampersand specifies that it is a pointer to the variable that is passed to the function. This coincides exactly with the explanation of the ampersand (pointer to) operator given in this chapter. The programmer's role in dealing with the pointer aspects of the parameter ceases at this point. The function accesses the value of the variable and changes its value as appropriate – using the pointer. This is carried out invisibly by the C++ system.

You will remember that when an array is passed as a reference parameter to a function, the programmer does not have to place an ampersand in front of the parameter name in the function header. This is because, in C++, arrays are always passed by reference (whether they are value or reference parameters). The reason for this is to save the space that would be needed to make a copy of an array. (Parameter passing in the language C is much more cumbersome than in C++ and it is described in Appendix F.)

What's the point?

Using pointers needs a good deal of clear thinking – and it may also seem to be unnecessarily cumbersome to the reader. So when and how are pointers used in C++ programs? There are four areas of application:

- parameter passing, as we have seen
- in conjunction with strings (see Chapter 15)
- to create and manipulate dynamic data structures (this is beyond the scope of this book)
- when it is important to speed up a program, because pointers provide 'shortcut' access (this is also beyond the scope of this book).

New language elements

* means 'item pointed to by'
& means 'pointer to'

Summary

- A pointer is a variable that contains a pointer to another variable.
- A pointer variable is distinguished by placing an asterisk before the variable name in the declaration.
- The & operator obtains a pointer to a variable.
- The * operator enables access to an item pointed to by a variable.

Programming pitfalls

Programming with pointers is notoriously exacting. Be meticulously careful. Use diagrams to check your thinking.

Exercise

1 Key in, compile and run a very small program that uses pointers, like this one:

```
#include <iostream.h>

void main (void)
{
int i, j;
int * p1, * p2;

i = 66;
p1 = & i;
p2 = p1;
j = *p2;

cout << i << j;
}
```

Check that you understand what it does and how it works.

CHAPTER 15
Strings

Introduction

If you want to write a program that processes text of any kind – names and addresses, for example – you will need to use strings. A string is a sequence of characters, like this:

hello, how are you?

Character data (Chapter 6) is something of a disappointment, because only one character can be stored in a character variable. Strings provide the answer because a complete series of characters of any length can be stored in a string variable. If you were going to write a word processor or a program to process names and addresses or a program to analyze the works of William Shakespeare, you would probably choose to use strings.

In common with other types of variables, the sort of operations that need to be done on strings are:

- declare strings
- input and output strings
- compare one string with another.

There are, in addition, a number of actions that are special to strings:

- search a string for a particular character or group of characters
- join two strings together
- break up a string into two pieces.

All these operations on strings are carried out by using the functions that are stored in one of the libraries. The library of string functions is called, expectedly, string. It is a fairly standard library, available on all systems and providing the facilities described below.

In order to use any of the string functions from the library, it is essential to give the following include instruction at the head of the program:

```
#include <string.h>
```

As we shall see, strings of characters are actually stored in one-dimensional arrays of characters.

Declaring a string

A string is a series of characters, which may include letters, spaces and punctuation characters. A string is held in computer memory in an array of characters. There has to be some way of marking the end of a string of characters. If a full-stop (period) character was used to signal the end of a string, then we couldn't set up a string which had a full stop as a part of the string. The same is true of any other character that we might choose. The answer to this problem is that the end of a string is signalled by means of a special character that we would never want to display or type. This character is known as the null character. The way that the null character is written is as 0. This is the reverse backslash character followed by the character zero. Although we write this as a *pair* of characters, the null character is actually stored in the computer as a *single* character. For historical reasons, the null character is usually known as NUL.

So the string consisting of the words hello friend looks like this in an array in memory:

h	e	l	l	o		f	r	i	e	n	d	\0

To set up a string variable, we first need an array like this:

```
char name[5];
```

remembering that the number in square brackets is the length of the array. This array provides sufficient room for a string consisting of four characters, plus the NUL character.

An alternative way of setting up a string variable is to declare the string and give it a value all in one go:

```
char name[] = "Alex";
```

Notice that we do not need to say how long the string is – the compiler works it out and sets up an array that is sufficiently long. Nor do we need to place the NUL character at the end of the string – the compiler does this for us. Nonetheless, this declaration does cause an array to be set up in memory – in this case an array with five elements in it:

A	l	e	x	\0

Almost all of the operations associated with strings work in this way. They automatically deal with the NUL character at the end of strings, so we do not have to worry about it.

There is another way of setting up the same string that we had above. Given that we have declared:

```
char name[5];
```

we can place some characters in the array one by one:

```
name[0]='A';
name[1]='l';
name[2]='e';
name[3]='x';
name[4]='\0';
```

and we were careful to ensure that the string we want to set up (the word Alex) ends with the NUL character. Now no-one would normally put values into a string in this way, but it emphasizes what a string variable has to look like.

Notice also that there are two different kinds of quote symbol used above, single and double:

'e' means a single character

whereas:

"e" means a string consisting of the character e followed by the NUL character. It needs an array with two elements in it for storage

Input and output of strings

We saw early on in this book how to output some text to the screen like this:

```
cout << "Hello, how are you?";
```

We can similarly use cout to display the contents of a string variable:

```
char name[] = "Alex";
cout << name;
```

which will display the name Alex on the screen.

We can also do more exotic things:

```
char name[] = "Mary";
cout << "Hello" << name << endl;
```

If we want to input a series of characters from the keyboard, we will have to set up a string variable that is sufficiently long to accommodate the string:

```
char name[20];
```

Then we can use `cin` to input a string:

```
cin >> name;
```

When `cin` is used to input a string:

1 It first skips any spaces that are input.
2 Then it reads characters from the keyboard until a space, newline or tab is reached.
3 The input stops and a NUL character is placed at the end of the string.

The space, newline or tab is not placed in the string variable.

If you remember, this works just like the input of a number – digits are input until a space, newline or tab is reached.

We can now enact a little dialogue:

```
char name[20];

cout << "What is your name?" << endl;
cin >> name;
cout << "hello" << name << endl;
```

Now there is a problem, of course, if someone has a particularly long name – or one that is longer than the array that is available. What happens? The answer is that disaster strikes. The input will take place relentlessly, overwriting whatever is in computer memory until the end of the input is encountered. So it is vital to declare a string variable that is sufficiently long. Other strategies are discussed below.

We have seen how to input a series of characters up to a space. But what if we want to input a name in two parts like the following?

Alice Butcher

If we use `cin` as above, we will only be able to input the first part of the name. One approach is to declare two string variables, one for the first name and one for the last name:

```
char first_name[20], last_name[20];

cin >> first_name;
cin >> last_name;
```

SELF-TEST QUESTION
A date in the form:

28 June 2015

is to be input into the computer. There is a space between each of the items in the date. Write C++ statements to input the three components of a date into three distinct string variables.

Another technique is to use an alternative library function called cin.getline, which inputs a complete line (up to a newline) and places it in the specified string variable:

```
char whole_line[80];

cin.getline (whole_line, 80);
```

The second parameter specifies the maximum number of characters that we want the function to input. This function inputs any characters, including spaces, up to a newline character. It places the string in the string variable, followed by the NUL character. The newline character is not placed in the string variable.

Notice that in this case, getline will not input more than 79 characters. The array that is provided has capacity for 80 characters, but there has to be sufficient room for the NUL terminating character.

getline is a very safe function to use when inputting strings, because it does check to make sure that it does not overfill the string variable.

Comparing strings

Comparing values is an important part of programming and we need to be able to compare two strings to see whether they are the same or not. As with other variable types, we do this using if, while and for statements. The library function strcmp compares two strings. Thus:

```
char one_word[2], another_word[20];

cin >> one_word >> another_word;
if (strcmp(one_word, another_word) == 0)
    cout << "they are the same";
else
    cout << "they are different";
```

strcmp compares the two strings and returns an integer as the value of the function:

- If the number is zero, the two strings are identical.
- If the two strings are different, strcmp returns a non-zero value.

SELF-TEST QUESTION

Write a piece of program that inputs a name from the keyboard and compares it with the name 'Charles'. If the name is the same, the program outputs 'You are famous'. Otherwise it outputs 'You are a nerd'.

Suppose we want a program to input words from the keyboard until the word amen is encountered. We will count how many words there are in the text. We need a loop that ends when the word is input.

```
char word[20];
int count;

count=0;
cin >> word;
while ( strcmp(word, "amen") != 0 )
    {
    count++;
    cin >> word;
    }
```

We can also use strcmp to put things in alphabetical order because:

- if the first parameter is before the second in the alphabet, strcmp returns a negative number (a number less than zero)
- if the first parameter is after the second in the alphabet, strcmp returns a positive number (a number greater than zero).

Thus we can compare two words like this:

```
char word1[20], word2[20];

cin >> word1 >> word2;

if (strcmp(word1, word2) < 0)
    cout << word1 << "is alphabetically before" << word2;
else
    cout << word2 << "is alphabetically before" << word1;
```

Copying strings

To copy the value of a string from one string variable to another we can use function strcpy, so that:

```
char From_here[20];
```

```
char To_here[20];
```

```
strcpy (To_here, From_here);
```

which copies the second string to the first string – it works right to left. The terminator, NUL, is copied as well.

The function strcpy does what an assignment statement does with simpler variables, like integers and single characters. With an integer, we can write:

```
int a, b;
a = b;
```

but doing a similar thing with strings is not allowed:

```
char a[10], b[10];
a = b; // illegal C++
```

We can also use strcopy to give a value to a string:

```
char name[20];
```

```
strcopy (name, "Bill Gates");
```

The analogous operation with integers is:

```
int number;
number = 42;
```

What happens if you copy a string but the receiving string is too short? The answer is a disaster! The string copy function remorselessly copies as many characters as there are in the second string (plus the terminating NUL). Whatever is stored in memory after the string variable (the array) will be changed.

Finding the length of a string

The library contains a number of useful functions to manipulate strings. As we have begun to see, the names of all of these functions start with the abbreviation str.

To find out how long a string is we can use strlen, which calculates the length of a string (not including the terminator, NUL), so that we can write:

```
char greeting[] = "How are you?";
int how_long;
```

```
how_long = strlen (greeting);
```

`strlen` returns an integer as the value of the function, in this case 12.

SELF-TEST QUESTION
Write a program that inputs any name from the keyboard and displays how long the name is.

Searching strings

It is common to want to search a string for some particular character or for some group of characters. The library functions `strchr`, `strrchr` or `strstr` can be used here. (Note the confusingly similar spellings of these names!)

Suppose, for example, we have a list of people that we want to invite to a party. We will put the list in a string:

```
char party = "Tom Dick Harriet Alice";
```

We will write a piece of program that inputs a name and checks to see if it is in the party list:

```
char name[2];
if (strstr(party, name) == NUL)
    cout << "sorry";
else
    cout << "welcome";
```

The function `strstr` searches the string which is its first parameter for the presence of the string which is its second parameter. It returns NUL if the required string is not in the string being searched.

As another example, suppose that we have a number of records of people's personal details. Each such record has a format like this:

Mike Bower:7.5.68:programmer:40000

which consists of a name, a date of birth, a job title and a salary, separated by colon characters. A typical operation would be to examine one of these fields of information. Suppose, for example, that we needed the information about the date of birth.

It is at this stage in studying strings that the reader needs to know something about pointers, which was the subject of Chapter 14. Using pointers needs new concepts, care and particularly clear thinking. If you skip to the start of the next section, on joining and dividing strings, you need not worry about pointers.

We can use the string search function to search for the colon character, isolate the required field and extract it. The code, annotated with detailed comments, is as follows. A commentary is given afterwards.

```
// the information about the person
char personal_details[]= "Mike Bower:7.5.68:programmer:
  40000";
// a pointer ready to point to the start of the date of birth
  field
char *begin[];
// a pointer ready to point to the end of the date of birth
  field
char *end[];
// a string ready to hold the date of birth information
char date_of_birth[10];

// search the string for a colon character
begin = strchr (personal_details, ':');
// increment the pointer past the colon
begin++;
// search the string again for a colon character
end = strchr (begin, ':');
// place NUL at the end of the date of birth field
*end = NUL;
// copy the date of birth information out of the original string
strcpy (date_of_birth, begin);
// output the required information
cout << "The date of birth is" << date_of_birth;
```

The above steps are:

1   The function `strchr` searches for the presence of a single character, in this case the colon. The function returns a pointer to the first occurrence of the colon character. This is a pointer to the colon immediately preceding the date of birth information.
2   The pointer is incremented so that it points to the first character of the required information, the date of birth.
3   `strchr` is used again to find the colon at the end of the date of birth information. A pointer to this colon is placed in variable end.
4   The character pointed to by pointer end (which was a colon) is replaced by the NUL character, making it the end of a string.
5   The date of birth information is copied from its field within the personal details string into the string called date_of_birth.
6   Finally the date of birth is output.

This sequence of coding is rich in detail, particularly because it uses pointers.

SELF-TEST QUESTION
Write the code to extract the job title of the person from the record.

The third function in the library collection, `strrchr`, searches for the *last* occurrence of a single character in a string. (See Appendix B for details.)

Joining and dividing strings

Joining one string on to the end of another is known as concatenation. The library function `strcat` does this.

If for example we have two string variables:

```
char first[50];
char second [] = "you won't be sorry!";
```

and we place some text in the first:

```
strcpy(first, "Are you sure");
```

then:

```
strcat (first, second);
cout << first;
```

gives the output:

```
Are you sure you won't be sorry!
```

The string second is added to the end of the string first. The first string is changed but the second is left intact. The terminating character is placed at the end of the new, extended string.

If the first string variable is too short to accommodate the lengthened string, disaster will strike, since no checking is carried out. The place in memory after the string variable will be corrupted.

Summary

- A string is a series of characters, including letters, spaces and punctuation characters.
- A string is stored in a one-dimensional array of characters, and terminated by the null character, denoted \0.

Exercises

1 Write a program to carry out the following dialogue, but with any name:

```
please enter your name:
Doug
hello Doug
```

2 Write a program that inputs a name from the keyboard and tests it to see if it is a famous name. Choose two names (say Charles and Diana) as names that are famous and that you will use in the program for comparison.

3 Write a program to input words from the keyboard and count how many words there are. The words end with the word 'goodbye'.

4 Write a program to input some text and calculate the average word length.

5 Write a program to input some text and calculate the number of occurrences of the popular letter e. Calculate the percentage occurrence of the letter e.

6 Write a program to input a word from the keyboard and decide whether it is a palindrome, that is whether it is the same spelled backwards. Thus, for example, madam is a palindrome, but the word hello is not.

7 Suppose that the library function `strlen` does not exist. Write the function.

8 Write a program that inputs words and displays their plurals according to the following rules:

   normally, add the letter s to the end of the word
   if the word ends in s, replace it with es

9 Write a program to input a line of text, and output it again, replacing every occurrence of the word 'a' by the word 'the'.

10 Write a program to play the game of hangman. The computer first inputs a word. Then the human player has to guess the word, by guessing one character at a time. After a guess, the computer displays the partially guessed word in the form:

```
e*e*h*n*
```

If the human gets all the words with five guesses then he or she is the winner. Otherwise, the computer wins.

11 The game of consequences is usually played with pencil and paper. This version uses the computer. Write a program that solicits input by means of a sequence of prompts and then displays a little encounter.
   The prompts from the computer are as follows:

```
Give me a man's name:
```

```
Give me a woman's name:
Give me a place:
What did he say?
What did she say?
What happened at the end?
```

Then the computer displays the complete story, which might be:

```
Mickey Mouse met Madonna at St Paul's Cathedral. He said
'What's a nice girl like you doing in a place like this?
She said 'Come up and see me some time'. And the
consequence was that they lived happily ever after.
```

CHAPTER 16

File processing

Introduction

Computer memory is usually measured in bytes. A single byte holds an individual character – a letter, a space, punctuation symbol or digit. A page of text with 40 lines and 20 characters per line therefore needs 800 bytes of storage. The main memory of a personal computer is usually several million bytes (megabytes). It may sound a lot of memory, but it easily gets filled with programs.

Space is usually much more plentiful on a disk. A hard disk will typically hold tens or hundreds of megabytes.

Another difference between main memory and disks is that disk space is much cheaper – measured in pence per byte.

Yet another difference between main memory and disk is that data stored on a disk is fairly permanent. Data in main memory vanishes when you switch off the computer and is therefore rather vulnerable.

To sum up:

- disk space memory is cheaper
- disk storage is permanent; data in main memory is temporary
- access to main memory is faster than access to disk.

The bottom line is that if you have a lot of information and you want to keep it, store it on a disk.

Information stored on a disk is kept in files, just as humans store information in files in a filing cabinet. A file holds a collection of related information. For example:

- a letter
- a graphics image
- the sales of computers in the UK, by region, over 10 years
- the source code of a program
- the scores of your favourite football team.

A file has a name, given to it by its user or users. Like variable names in a program, file names have to be unique.

A collection of programs called the filing system manages the files on your disk(s). Usually a filing system allows you to collect a group of related files together in what is called a directory. Each directory has a name.

A case study

Suppose we want to create a file that holds the scores of our favourite football team. (If you're not interested in football, then think of a sport of your choice.) In order to avoid favouritism, we will choose the scores of a non-English team – AC Milan of Italy. For each match we want to hold the following information:

> date, away or home (a or h), our score, their score

We will need a whole series of lines of information, to record a whole season's scores. For example:

```
23 02 96 a 2 0
12 03 96 h 3 2
22 03 96 a 6 0
```

The easiest way to create the file and to put some information in it is to use a text editor. We will need some way of indicating the last entry in the file; to do this we will use as the value of the date 99 99 99.

There are several things that we might want to do to the file:

- create the file in the first place
- display the complete file on the screen
- display an individual result on the screen
- add a new result to the end of the file
- (occasionally) alter an existing result.

All of these things can be done using the text editor. However, what we want to do is to develop a special C++ program to carry out these operations.

SELF-TEST QUESTION
Devise a line of data for the file.

Input, output, reading and writing

Let us first clarify the jargon about accessing a file. Information in a file is input to the computer and placed in variables in just the same way that information is input from the keyboard. This is called reading or inputting from a file. The opposite is outputting (or writing) information from variables to a file.

Displaying a file

Suppose that we have already set a file containing the football score information described above. What we now want to do is to construct a program that displays the entire contents of the file on the screen.

Starting at the beginning of the file, the program will read the data and display it on the screen. The program will stop reading when it encounters the impossible date 99 99 99. The appropriate programming structure is a loop, and the `while` statement is a suitable way to do this.

The functions of the filing system are stored in a system library, and the header file `fstream.h` must be included at the top of a program that uses the functions.

Before a program can start to access a file, it has to call a library function to 'open' the file. This is analogous to opening the drawer of a filing cabinet and finding the file within the drawer. The program must supply the name of the particular file that it wants to use.

To use a file, the programmer has to declare a new kind of variable. We have already seen that variables of type `int`, `float` and `char` can be declared and used by a program. To input from a file, we have to declare a variable of type `ifstream`. This is short for input file stream. It is the variable that the file system and the program use to refer to the file. (It is not the same as the actual file name, which is given in the call to the function `open`.)

Here is a complete program to read information from the file and display it on the screen:

```
#include <iostream.h>
#include <fstream.h>
int main (void)
{
    ifstream football;

    int day, month, year;
    char place;
    int us, them;

    football.open ("milan", ios::in);

    football >> day >> month >> year >> place >> us >> them;
    while (day != 99)
    {
        cout << day << month << year << place << us << them;

        cout << endl;
        football >> day >> month >> year >> place >> us >>
          them;

    }

    football.close();
}
```

When the program has ceased using a file, it should call the library function `close`, to inform the filing system that the file is no longer in use. This is like a human user of a file closing the drawer of the filing cabinet.

SELF-TEST QUESTION
Create a small file of the football information using your text editor. Then run the above program and verify that it reads and displays the information correctly.

Creating a file

One way to create a file is to use the text editor. Suppose, however, that instead we want to write a special program to do it. We will input data on football scores from the keyboard and output it to the file. The end of the data is signified, as before, by the date 99 99 99. The coding is given below. Note that to output to a file, we have to declare a variable of type `ofstream` (output file stream) and then call the open function with a parameter that specifies that it will be used for output.

```
#include <iostream.h>
#include <fstream.h>
int main (void)
{
     ofstream football;

     int day, month, year;
     char place;
     int us, them;

     football.open ("milan", ios::out);

     cin >> day >> month >> year >> place >> us >> them;
     while (day != 99)
     {
         football << day << month << year << place <<
           us << them << endl;
         cin >> day >> month >> year >> place >> us >> them;
     }
     football << day << month << year << place << us << them;

     football.close();
}
```

This program is careful not to forget to output the end of file information (with a value of day equal to 99) to the new file.

SELF-TEST QUESTION
Run the above program in order to create a new file. Make sure that you do not destroy
any file that you have already created, because creating a file will obliterate any
information that was in the file beforehand. Check that it has been created correctly by
examining it with your text editor.

End of file

In the program we have written above, the programmer has marked the end of the
information by means of a special data value. Because this is a very common thing
to want to do, the filing system provides its own way of marking the end of a file.
The filing system attaches information to the file to say where its end is, and
provides the facility for the program to test for the end of the file.

The program can test to see whether the end of a file has been reached by testing
the value of the file variable. If the value is zero, then the end of the file has been
reached. So we can write:

```
ifstream football;

if (football == 0) cout << "end of file reached";
```

When a program creates a file by outputting information to it, the filing system
automatically attaches the end of file information when the program calls the
close function.

The code for the program to display the football information, using the end of
file is:

```
#include <iostream.h>
#include <fstream.h>
int main (void)
{
    ifstream football;

    int day, month, year;
    char place;
    int us, them;

    football.open ("milan", ios::in);

    while (football != 0)
    {
        football >> day >> month >> year >> place >> us
            >> them;
```

```
        cout << day << month << year << place << us << them;

        cout << endl;
    }
    football.close();
}
```

SELF-TEST QUESTION
Run this program. When this works correctly, you may find that you wish to delete the
special end of file line with the meaningless day value of 99.

Adding to a file

As the football results come in, week by week, we want to add new information to
the end of the file of football results. This is termed appending information. The
program to carry out this task needs to create a variable of type ofstream and
then open the file, not as input or output, but as 'app'.

The program then simply outputs the new information, which is appended to the
existing information in the file:

```
#include <iostream.h>
#include <fstream.h>
int main (void)
{
    ofstream football;

    int day, month, year;
    char place;
    int us, them;

    football.open ("milan", ios::app);

    cin >> day >> month >> year >> place >> us >> them;
    football << day << month << year << place << us <<
       them << endl;

    football.close();
}
```

SELF-TEST QUESTION
Again, run this program and check that it has correctly appended a new line of
information to the end of the file by examining the lengthened file using your text editor.

Updating a file

What sort of changes might we want to make to the file of football data? Here are some possibilities:

- add the result of a recent match to the end of the file
- change one of the results within the file (which was entered incorrectly for some reason)
- add a new result within the middle of the file (which was omitted by mistake)
- delete a result from the middle of the file (which was too shameful to leave).

Each of these changes means an update to the file.

We have already seen how to add (append) information to the end of a file. This is the only kind of change to a file that is allowed. This may seem strange, and unduly restrictive, but it is true. There are other types of file that can be changed (see later), but serial files cannot be changed – except by adding information at the end.

Serial files

The file of football results is called a serial file. Serial files have the following characteristics:

- They can only be read (input) by starting at the beginning of the file and inputting item by item, until the end of the file is reached.
- The information within the file cannot be changed (except to append information at the end of the file).

This second feature may seem catastrophic – what's the use of a file that you can't change? But in practice there are many applications in which a file is first created and then never changed. Examples are the machine code version of a C++ program, the image of a computer graphic. In both these examples, if the file needs to be changed, then it is re-written as a whole.

If it is necessary to change a serial file, then it can be done by copying the file. For example, suppose we want to insert some additional information into a serial file. We first copy the file, creating a new file up to the insertion point, then output the new information to the file, and finally copy the remainder of the file.

SELF-TEST QUESTION
Give two differences between arrays and serial files.

Random files

C++ provides facilities for handling types of files other than serial files. The most important file type is a random access file. Such a file has the following properties:

- Access (reading) can be made immediately to the position of some desired information in the file. It is not necessary (as with serial files) to start at the beginning and read through the file, line by line. This means that access is very fast.
- New information can be inserted anywhere within the file. This means that it is very easy to update a random access file.

As we have seen, neither of these facilities is possible with serial files.
An explanation of random access file handling is beyond the scope of this book.

Summary

- A file is a collection of related information. Each file has its own name.
- Information is input (read) from a file into variables in main memory. Information is output (written) from variables in main memory to a file.
- The relationship between the program and the filing system is via a variable called a file stream variable, declared in a similar fashion to a data item.
- Before information in a file is accessed, the program must issue a call to the library function open, giving the file name and the way in which it is to be used (input, output or append).
- When a program has ceased to use a file it should issue a call to the library function close.
- A serial file is processed by reading (or writing) information starting at the beginning of the file and continuing item by item along the file.

Exercises

General

Implement the football results programs and check that they work satisfactorily.

Game

Enhance one of the games you have written so that it maintains a list of the high scorers in a file on a disk. Such a list gives the names and best scores ever of the game, like this:

Ali 40000
Jim 37000
Mar 36000

Display the scores at the start of each game. Check the scores at the end of each game and amend the file if necessary.

Information system

Write a program to provide a personal telephone directory. It should provide the following options:

given a name, display the number
display the complete directory
add a new entry
change an existing entry

CHAPTER 17

Debugging

Introduction

Debugging is the name given to the job of finding out where the bugs are in a program. After you have keyed in a program, you usually have to spend some considerable time getting rid of the compilation errors. Eventually the program compiles 'cleanly'. Then, at last, the program runs. But it is very unusual for it to work as expected. In fact it is usual for the program to fail in some way or behave in a way other than was intended. You have a bug in the program – or more likely many bugs! So you have to carry out some debugging.

The term bug originated in the days of valve computers, when (allegedly) a large insect became lodged in the circuitry of an early computer, causing it to malfunction. Hence the term 'bug' and the term 'debugging'.

The problem with debugging is that the symptoms of a bug are usually very meagre. So we have to resort to detective work to find the cause.

Once the more obvious faults in a program have been eliminated, it is usual to start carrying out some systematic testing. Testing is the repeated running of a program with a variety of data as input. It is discussed in Chapter 18. The aim of testing is to convince the world that the program works properly. But normally testing reveals more bugs. So testing and debugging go hand in hand.

> **SELF-TEST QUESTION**
> What is the difference between debugging and testing?

Many programmers like debugging; they see it as exciting – like watching a mystery thriller in which the villain is revealed only at the last moment. Certainly, along with testing, debugging often takes a long time. Do not be worried that debugging takes you some time – this is normal!

Debugging

A program runs but behaves unexpectedly. How do we find the source of the problem? Because a program runs invisibly, we need something like x-ray specs to gain some insight into how the program is behaving. This is the key to successful debugging – getting additional information about the running program.

One way to obtain additional information is to insert extra output (`cout`) statements in the program. The trick is to choose the best points in the program. Generally, good points to choose are:

- just before a call to a function (to check that the parameters are OK)
- just after a call to a function (to check that the function has done its work correctly).

Using a debugger

The C++ system that you are using will probably come with a 'debugger'. A debugger is a program that helps you debug your program. It runs alongside your program, allowing the progress of the program to be inspected. It will provide several facilities. Unfortunately debuggers are not standardized, and therefore this book cannot explain the facilities in detail.

Using a debugger, the programmer can place a *breakpoint* in the program. A breakpoint is a place in the program where execution stops. When a breakpoint is reached, the debugger allows the values of variables to be inspected to see if they are what they should be. Any discrepancy provides information for debugging.

With *tracing*, the debugger lets us see the program execute in slow motion so that we can check that it is taking the expected path. Pausing allows us to inspect values of variables. A useful version of tracing is *single-shotting*, in which the computer executes just one C++ instruction at a time before pausing.

Common errors in C++ programs

Some errors are commonly made by C++ programmers. It is worth while checking any program for these errors. These errors will *not* produce a compilation error – the program will run but exhibit strange behaviour.

Initialization

Failure to initialize a variable (remember that integers are *not* initialized to zero automatically).

Conditions

Using = instead of == in a condition. This coding:

```
if (a=b)   should be   if (a==b)
```

Function calling

Writing a function call on a function called doIt like this:

```
doIt;   rather than   doIt();
```

and will result in the function call being ignored.

Array subscripts

If an array is declared as:

```
int array[10];
```

then the following for loop will incorrectly use the 10th element of the array:

```
for (s=0; s<= 10; s++)
    array[s]=0;
```

Parameter passing

In a function heading, if you omit the & alongside a parameter which is to be changed by the function, it will not get changed. For example, this will not do what you expect:

```
void assign (int a, int b)
{
    b=a;
}
```

Summary

- Debugging is finding errors (bugs) in a program.
- Some C++ systems provide a 'debugger' program that can assist with debugging.
- A breakpoint is a place where the program temporarily stops to permit inspection of the values of variables.
- Tracing is watching the execution flow through the program.

CHAPTER 18

Testing

Introduction

Programs are complex and it is difficult to make them work correctly. Testing is one set of techniques that can be used to attempt to verify that a program does work correctly.

The starting point for any testing is the specification. Time is never wasted in studying and clarifying the specification. Take the following specification, for example:

> Write a program that inputs a series of numbers. The numbers are terminated by a negative number. Calculate and print the sum of the numbers.

On first reading, this specification may look simple and clear. But, even though it is so short, it contains pitfalls:

- Are the numbers integers or floating points?
- Is the negative number to be included in the sum, or not?
- Should the answer be printed, or should it be displayed on the screen?

These questions should be clarified before the programmer starts any programming. Indeed it is part of the job of programming to study the specification, discover any omissions or confusion, and gain agreement to a clear specification. After all, it is no use writing a brilliant program if it doesn't do what the client wanted.

Here now is a pristine version of the specification, which we will use as a case study in looking at testing methods:

> Write a program that inputs a series of integers. The integers are in the range 0 to 10,000. The numbers are terminated by a negative number. Calculate and display the sum of the numbers. The negative number is not to be included in the sum.

Exhaustive testing

One approach to testing would be to test a program with all possible data values as input.

Consider the program to input a series of numbers. There could be one, two or 10,000 numbers. Each number has an enormously large range of possible values.

All in all, the number of possible combinations of numbers is fantastic. All the different values would have to be keyed in and the program run repetitively. The human time taken to assemble the test data would be years. Even the time that the computer (fast as they are) needs would be days. Finally, checking that the computer had got the answers correct would drive someone mad.

Thus exhaustive testing – even for a small and simple program – is not feasible. Therefore we have to adopt some other approach.

Black box testing

Knowing that exhaustive testing is infeasible, the 'black box' approach to testing is to devise sample data that is representative of all possible data. Then we run the program, input the data and see what happens.

Black box testing is so known because no knowledge of the workings of the program is used as part of the testing. The program is thought of as being invisible within a black box.

For the program to add up the series of numbers, we need some representative data. Being bold, we might argue that any integer is typical of any other integer. Also, two pieces of data are representative of any number of pieces of data. Thus we choose one set of test data:

8   12   −99

and the testing is complete!

Nervously, we might worry that this is too limited. We might argue that to have no numbers is special and that therefore we should also test with the data:

−99

Worried still that this testing is inadequate, we might argue that the number 0, as a piece of input data, is special and that therefore we should also test the program with:

8   0   12   −99

which completes the testing according to the black box approach.

SELF-TEST QUESTION
A program's function is to input three integer numbers and find the largest. Devise black box test data for this program.

SELF-TEST QUESTION
In a program to play the game of chess, the player specifies the destination for a move as a pair of subscripts, the row and column number. The program checks that the destination square is valid – that is, not outside the board. Devise black box test data to check that this part of the program is working correctly.

White box testing

White box testing makes use of knowledge of how a program works – it uses the listing of the program code. The knowledge of how the program works is used as the basis of devising test data. Then we run the program, input the data and see what happens.

Here is the code for the program we are using as a case study:

```
#include <iostream.h>

int main(void)
{
    int sum, number;

    sum=0;
    cin >> number;
    while (number>=0)
        {
        sum=sum+number;
        cin >> number;
        }
    cout << sum;
}
```

The principle of white box testing is that every statement in the program should be executed at some time during the testing. In our sample program, it is obvious how to do this, but in large, complex programs it may not be as easy.

Using the test data:

8   0   12   −99

will make sure that every statement is executed. It will also check that the condition in the while works as desired in different circumstances.

Sparse as this test data is, it seems to fulfil objective criteria for white box testing. To illustrate how fallible this data is, however, suppose that the statement:

```
sum=0;
```

had been left out of the program, presumably in error. Would the testing reveal this error? The answer is that it might or might not. If the memory allocated to the variable sum happened to contain zero, then the program would work correctly when it was tested and might therefore be assumed to be correct. However, it might well be that on a different occasion the memory does not contain zero, so the program will work incorrectly.

SELF-TEST QUESTION

A program's function is to input three numbers and find the largest. Devise white box test data for this program.

The code is:

```
int a, b, c;

cin >> a >> b >> c;

if (a > b)
    if (a > c) cout << a
        else cout << c;
else
    if (b > c) cout << b
        else cout << c;
```

SELF-TEST QUESTION

In a program to play the game of chess, the player specifies the destination for a move as a pair of subscripts, the row and column number. The program checks that the destination square is valid – that is, not outside the board. Devise white box test data to check that this part of the program is working correctly.

The code for this part of the program is:

```
int row, col;

cin >> row >> col;

if ((row > 8) || (row < 1)) cout << "error";
if ((col > 8) || (col < 1)) cout << "error";
```

Inspection

There is one method that doesn't make use of a computer at all in trying to eradicate faults in a program. It is called inspection. In an inspection, someone simply studies the program listing (along with the specification) in order to try to see bugs. It is better that the person doing the inspecting is not the person who wrote the program. This is because people tend to be blind to their own errors. It is extraordinary to witness how quickly someone else sees an error that has been defeating you for hours!

The evidence from controlled experiments suggests that inspections are a very effective way of finding errors.

Conclusion

There isn't a fool-proof testing method that will ensure that programs are free of errors. The best approach would be to use a combination of testing methods – black box and white box – together with inspection. To use all three methods would, however, be very time consuming. So we need to exercise considerable judgement and skill to decide what sort of testing to do and how much testing to do.

Testing is a frustrating business – because we know that, however patient and systematic we are, we can never be sure that we have done enough. Testing requires massive patience, attention to detail and organization.

Summary

- Testing is a technique, that is it tries to ensure that a program is free from errors.
- Testing cannot be exhaustive because there are just too many cases.
- Black box testing uses only the specification to choose test data.
- White box testing uses a knowledge of how the program works in order to choose test data.
- Inspection simply means studying the program listing in order to find errors.

Exercise

1 Devise black box and white box test data to test the following program. The program specification is:

The program inputs a series of integers from the keyboard. The numbers are terminated with the number −999. The program finds the largest of the numbers.

The program code is:

```
#include <iostream.h>

int main (void)
{
int n, largest;

cin >> n;
largest = n;
while (n != -999)
```

```
        {
        if (n > largest) largest = n;
        cin >> n;
        }
    cout << largest;
    }
```

CHAPTER 19

Piecemeal programming

Introduction

Even the most experienced programmers cannot write a program and get it working properly straightaway. A long period of debugging and testing is the norm in programming. This can be very frustrating for novices. This chapter is about a technique for helping to avoid these frustrations.

One approach to writing a program is to write the whole program, key it in and try to compile it. The keyword here is 'try', because most programmers find that their friendly compiler will find lots of errors on the occasion of the first compilation of their program. It can be very disheartening – particularly for novices – to see so many error messages decorating a program that was the result of so much effort. Once the compilation errors have been banished, the program usually will exhibit strange behaviours during the (sometimes lengthy) period of debugging and testing.

An alternative is piece-by-piece programming – usually called *incremental* programming. The steps are:

1   write a small piece of the program
2   key it in, compile it, run it and debug it
3   add a new, small piece of the program
4   repeat from step 2 until the program is complete.

The trick is to identify the pieces of the program – and these are usually functions.

We will see how to put these steps into practice using two examples.

Case study – a game

To illustrate incremental programming, we will demonstrate how a game program could be developed. It actually doesn't matter which game program it is, because during the early stages of the development of this program, one game looks very much like another. However, the particular game is the game of Nim.

Nim is a game played with matchsticks (unused or used). It doesn't matter how many matches there are. The matches are put into three piles. Again, it doesn't matter how many matches there are in each pile. Each player goes in turn. A player can remove any number of matches from any one pile, but only one pile. A player must remove at least one match. The winner is the person who causes the other player to take the last match.

In the computer version of the game, there are two players, the computer and the human. The computer plays by selecting a pile and a number of matches randomly.

We will provide the facility to play a number of games, until the human gets tired. After one game is played, the program asks the player:

```
quit? y or n?
```

to which the human responds appropriately.

There is clearly a loop here, which constitutes the main part of the program. So we can start to write the program like this:

```
#include <iostream.h>

int main (void)
{
    char response;
    void play_nim (void);

    response='n';
    while (response != 'y');
        {
        play_nim();
        cout << "quit? y or n?" << endl;
        cin >> response;
        }
}
```

We resist the temptation to write much more of the program, simply coding the function called play_nim as:

```
void play_nim (void)
{
    cout << "Play a game of Nim" << endl;
}
```

This is called stub. It plainly doesn't do the real job that play_nim should do. It pretends to do the job, by outputting a message. A stub is a function that temporarily substitutes for the real thing. It allows the program to be compiled successfully and indeed to run.

We can key in and run this cut-down version of the final program. We can eliminate any compile-time errors easily, because the program is so short. It will run, giving this appearance:

```
Play a game of Nim
quit? y or n?
n
Play a game of Nim
quit? y or n?
y
```

The great virtue of doing this is that not only can we remove a number of errors easily but we can see a working program. This will give us confidence.

The story continues. We write the function play_nim. We make it short. We make it use a number of subsidiary functions. These we implement as simple stubs. We compile and run again, eliminating any bugs. The code for play_nim is:

```
void play_nim (void)
{
        void get_matches (void);
        void create_heaps (void);
        void take_a_turn (void);
        void declare_the_winner (void);

        get_matches ();
        create_heaps ();
        while (count > 0)
               take_a_turn ();
        declare_the_winner ();
}
```

with the variable count declared as an integer in the global data at the head of the program.

We continue like this, adding new functions one by one and debugging them, until the complete program is assembled. At each stage, there will be few errors to eliminate.

Case study – a calculator

Here is another illustration of piece-by-piece programming, this time applied to a rather different program, taken from one of the exercises in an earlier chapter.

A program is to input a series of numerical data values into an array. The numbers are in the range 0 to 100. The numbers are terminated with some special value – say a negative number.

The program is to calculate:

the largest number

the smallest number
the sum of the numbers
the mean of the numbers .

Finally the program is to display a histogram that shows how many numbers are in
the ranges 0 to 9, 10 to 19, 20 to 29, etc.

As can be seen, the program has a number of different tasks to carry out. This
makes it a particularly suitable candidate for incremental implementation.

The first step is to construct the smallest of programs to input the numbers, place
them in the array and output them. This checks that the input is working and that
the array is being used correctly:

```
int main (void)
{
     const int size = 100;
     int array[size];
     int number, length;

     void input_array(int array[], int & length);
     void display_array(int array[], int length);

     input_array(array, length);
     display_array(array, length);
}

void input_array(int array[], int & length)
{
     int number;

     cin >> number;
     while (number > 0)
         {
         array[length] = number;
         length++;
         cin >> number;
         }
}

void display_array(int array[], int length)
{
     int s;
     for (s=0; s<length; s++)
         cout << array[s];
}
```

This is quite long enough for a first implementation of the program. We would next insert the calls on the functions to find the smallest element in the array, to find the largest element, etc. The functions themselves would initially be stubs. Then we flesh out one of the stubs – say the one to find the smallest element in the array – key it in, compile and run. And so on.

Summary

- Piece-by-piece (incremental) programming is probably more effective than 'big-bang' programming.
- Write the main program first, leaving the other functions incomplete as stubs.
- Get the main program working properly to boost your confidence.
- Add functions one by one and get them working one by one.

Exercise

1   Why not try to use this technique in future when you embark on writing a new program?

CHAPTER 20

Program style

Introduction

Programming is a highly creative and exciting activity. Programmers often get very absorbed in their work and regard the programs that they produce as being very much their personal creations. The stereotypical programmer (man or woman) wears jeans and a T-shirt. He or she drinks 20 cups of coffee in a day and stays up all night just for the fun of programming.

The facts of programming life are rather different. Most programming is done within commercial organizations. Most programs are worked on by several different people. Many organizations have standards manuals that detail what programs should look like.

Most programs are read by several people – and certainly not just their author. The others are: the people who take on your work when you get promoted or move to another project, the people who will test your program and the generations of programmers who will look after your program, fixing bugs and making improvements long after you have got another job. So, making your program easy to read is a vital ingredient of programming.

Unless you are a hobbyist, it's important in practice, therefore, to know how to produce good programs.

Program layout

The C++ programmer has enormous scope in deciding how to lay out a program. The language is free format – new lines, spaces and new pages can be used almost anywhere. Comments can be placed on a line by themselves or on the end of a line of code. There's certainly plenty of scope for creativity and individuality.

However, as we have seen, most programs are read by several people other than the original author. So good appearance is vital. We will now look at a set of style guidelines for C++ programs. No doubt you, the reader, will disagree with some of them.

Names

In C++, the programmer gives names to variables and functions. There's plenty of scope for imagination because:

- names can consist of letters, digits and underlines
- names can be as long as you like

provided that:

- a name starts with a letter
- a name is unique somewhere in its first 32 characters.

The usual advice on names is to make them as meaningful as possible. This rules out cryptic names like i, j, x, y which usually signify that the programmer has some background in maths.

Indentation

Indentation emphasizes program structure. There are various styles for indentation, of which just one has been used throughout this book. People also disagree about how many spaces should be used for indentation – five are used in this book.

Blank lines

Blank lines are usually used to separate functions visually. They are also sometimes used within a function to separate the data declarations and function prototypes from the action part of a function.

Comments

There is great controversy about comments. Some people argue that the 'more the better'. However, sometimes you see code like this:

```
// display the result
cout << result;
```

in which the comment merely repeats the code, and is therefore superfluous.

Often the code is overwhelmed by suffocating comments which add little to the understanding of the code. It's like a Christmas tree that is overwhelmed with tinsel, baubles and lights. There is another problem: some studies have shown that, where there are a lot of comments, the reader reads the comments and ignores the code. Thus, if the code is wrong, it will remain so.

Some people argue that comments are needed when the code is complex or difficult to understand in some way. This seems reasonable until you wonder why the code needs to be complex. Sometimes, perhaps, the code can be simplified so that it is easy to understand without comments. We give example of such situations below.

Our conclusion is that perhaps comments should be used sparingly and judiciously.

Using constants

Many programs have values that do not change while the program is running – and don't change very often anyway! Examples are the VAT (Value-Added Tax) rate, the age for voting, the threshold for paying tax, mathematical constants. C++ provides the facility to declare data items as constants and give them a value. So, for the above examples, we can write:

```
const float VAT_rate = 17.5;
const int voting_age = 18;
const int tax_threshold = 5000;
const float pi = 3.142;
```

One benefit of doing this is that the compiler will detect any attempt (no doubt by mistake!) to change the value of a constant. Thus, for example:

```
voting_age = 17;
```

would provoke an error message.

Another, more powerful benefit is that a program that otherwise might be peppered with rather meaningless numbers, contains clear, meaningful quantities. This enhances program clarity, with all its consequent benefits.

Suppose, for example, we need to alter a tax program to reflect a change in regulations. We have a nightmare task if the tax thresholds and tax rates are built into the program as numbers that appear as-and-when throughout the program. We could use a text editor to search for all occurrences of what we understand a tax threshold to be, say 5000. The editor will dutifully tell us where all the occurrences are, but we are left unsure that this number has the same meaning everywhere. The answer, of course, is to use constants, with good names, and to distinguish carefully between different data items.

In C programming, it has always been the convention to use upper case (capital) letters for the names of constants. Thus, for example, the terminating character for strings is always known as NUL. Using upper case distinguishes these values from others in the program and makes it evident that they are indeed constants. Some people would like to preserve this convention and carry it over into C++ programming. We leave readers to judge for themselves.

Parameter passing

This book heavily emphasizes the use of functions as a means of promoting readability of the program. Along with functions goes parameter passing and, in the language C++, a variety of mechanisms for doing it:

- passing by value
- passing by reference
- returning a value as the value of the function
- using global data.

We want to rule out the last possibility immediately as poor style, and something that should only be used occasionally and with very good reason.

The custom in C++ programming, inherited from C programming, is that the return value is used to indicate the success (zero) or failure (non-zero) of the function. For example:

```
if (get_digit(digit)==0)
    process_digit(digit);
else
    cout << "Error. Non-digit in input";
```

Function size

It is possible to get into long and enjoyable arguments about how long a function should be.

One view is that a function should not be longer than a single page of listing. That way, we do not have to turn a page, or look at two pages, one alongside the other. We can thoroughly study the function, in its entirety. It is not so long that we lose track of some parts of it.

Grouping functions

A program of any useful size consists of a number of functions. In trying to read and understand a program it helps if functions that are related in some way are grouped together. Examples are:

- in a computer game, the functions that update and display the scores
- in a program with a user interface, the functions that deal with the user.

This sort of grouping is very much in line with modern ideas about modularity and object-oriented programming.

New pages

New pages can be used in conjunction with the layout of functions to enhance the readability of programs. Let us assume that no function is longer than a page, as suggested earlier. In one view, it is best to present each function on a page by itself.

This emphasizes the independence of each function from the others. It enables one function to be studied without the distracting presence of any others.

Perhaps one of the worst crimes in laying out a program is when a function starts on one page of listing but then spills over onto another. The concentration of the reader is broken by the end of the page and the start of the new one.

Function prototypes

Function prototypes advertise what functions are to be used, their names and their parameters. There are two schools of thought about where it is best to place function prototypes:

1   at the beginning of each function
2   at the beginning of the program.

This book adopts the first style – at the start of each function is a set of declarations saying what other functions the current function uses. This style tends to make each function self-contained. In order to understand each function, you only have to read the function itself; no other information outside the function is required. All the declarations relevant to the function are there within it – the parameters, the local data and the function prototypes.

The other style presents the reader of the program with the complete set of function prototypes at the head of the program. This is, in fact, a list of all of the functions in the program (except main). The reader can get a feel of the size of the program and the number of functions. This style of programming comes into its own when programs are much bigger than those considered in this book. Such programs consist of a number of files, each consisting of a number of functions. It is useful in such situations for the names of all the functions to appear at the head of the file, advertising their presence in the file.

We leave it to readers to choose and adopt a style that they prefer.

Nested if statements

Nesting is the term given to the situation in a program when there is a while loop within a while loop, or an if statement within an if statement. Generally, nesting is considered to be bad, and best avoided.

Let's look at nested if statements. Consider the problem of inputting three numbers and finding which is the largest:

```
cin >> a >> b >> c;

if (a>b)
    if (a>c)
```

```
            cout << a;
      else
            cout << c;
  else
      if (b>c)
            cout << b;
      else
            cout << c;
```

This is certainly a complicated-looking piece of program. In the author's experience, people usually have some trouble understanding it. They are not always convinced that it works correctly. So, on the evidence, it is difficult to read and understand. Arguably the complexity arises from the nesting of the if statements.

An alternative piece of program that avoids the nesting is:

```
cin >> a >> b >> c;

if (a>b && a>c) cout << a;
if (b>a && b>c) cout << b;
if (c>a && c>b) cout << c;
```

which is much clearer, we would all agree! The trouble with this solution is that all *three* if statements are always executed, whereas in the first program only *two* tests are performed. So the second program will run slightly slower. This is true in general – programs with nested if statements run faster.

Here's another example of nesting. In a game program the player controls the hero (or heroine) figure by using the keys n, s, e, w to move the hero north, south, east or west respectively. (These aren't actually very good keys to choose ergonomically, but that's not the issue here.) Within the program, the position of the hero is maintained as x and y co-ordinates in two variables, x and y. The program looks like this:

```
cin >> c;

if (c=='n') y++;
else
    if (c=='s') y--;
    else
        if (c=='e') x++;
        else
            x--;
```

where there is an if within an if within an if. This piece of program uses consistent indentation, but it's not too easy to understand it. Some people recommend laying out such a sequence like this:

```
cin >> c;

if (c=='n') y++;
else if (c=='s') y--;
else if (c=='e') x++;
else x--;
```

which is more compact, and makes it look as if there is an 'else if' facility in the language.

The other alternative is, of course, to code it without nesting:

```
cin >> c;

if (c=='n') y++;
if (c=='s') y--;
if (c=='e') x++;
if (c=='w') x--;
```

which is arguably much clearer. Again, the penalty is that the clearer program is slower – because all the if statements are always executed.

No doubt you, the reader, have seen that there is perhaps a resolution to this dilemma. We could re-code this piece of program using the switch statement as:

```
cin >> c;

switch (c)
    {
    case 'n' : y++; break;
    case 's' : y--; break;
    case 'e' : x++; break;
    case 'w' : x--; break;
    }
```

which is clear and fast. The problem is, however, that the switch statement is restricted; you can only use it to switch on the value of an integer or a character. So, for example, it cannot be used in the program above to find the largest of three numbers. Use of switch is not a general solution to the problem of nested if statements.

The conclusion is this: if you avoid nested if statements you may suffer a performance penalty. In practice, reduced performance will only matter if the test is

carried out inside a loop repeated many times within a program that is time critical
– like a program to control a power station.

Nested loops

Let us now look at nesting within loops. Suppose we are writing a piece of program
that displays a pattern like this on the screen:

```
FFFFFFFFF
FFFFFFFFF
FFFFFFFFF
FFFFFFFFF
FFFFFFFFF
```

which is a crude graphic of a block of flats (apartments). The piece of program
could look like this:

```
int flat, floor;

for (floor= 0; floor < 10; floor++)
    {
    for (flat=0; flat< 6; flat++)
        cout << "F";
    cout << endl;
    }
```

in which one for loop is nested within the other. This is not a particularly complex
piece of code, but we can simplify it using functions:

```
int floor;

for (floor= 0; floor < 10; floor++)
    {
    draw_floor();
    cout << endl;
    }
void draw_floor()
{
    int flat;

    for (flat=0; flat< 6; flat++)
        cout << "F";
}
```

Here we have eliminated the nesting. We have expressed explicitly in the coding the fact that the block of flats consists of a number of floors. We have clarified the requirement that there is one newline for each floor of the block.

Enhance the coding to draw the block of flats so that the number of floors and the number of flats on each floor are both variables. Pass as parameters the number of flats per floor and the number of floors.

Research studies have shown that we humans find it difficult to understand nesting. One researcher has summed this up by saying 'Nesting is for the birds'.

Complex conditions

A complex condition can make a program very difficult to understand, debug and get right. As an example, we will look at a program that searches an array of numbers to find a desired number:

```
int Table[100];

int wanted;
int i, length = 100;

i = 0;
while ( i<100 || Table[i]==wanted)
    i++;

if (i==100)
    cout << "not found";
else
    cout << "found";
```

The problem with this program is that the condition for the while is complex. Even for an experienced programmer it is difficult to check what has been written and to convince oneself that it is correct. There's an alternative. We will use something called a flag. It is just an integer variable, but its value at any time records the status of the search:

Initially it has value 0, meaning that the program is still searching
If and when the item is found, the value is made 1
If the search is completed without finding the item, the value is made 2

```
int Table[100];
```

```
int wanted;
int i, length = 100;
int searching;

i = 0;
while (searching==0)
    {
    if (wanted == Table[i]) searching = 1;
    i++;
    if (i == 100) searching = 2;
    }

if (searching == 2)
    cout << "not found";
else
    cout << "found";
```

What has been accomplished is that the various tests have been disentangled. The condition in the `while` loop is clear and simple. The other tests are separate and simple. The program overall is simpler.

Documentation

The old lavatorial saying is just as relevant to programming:

'The job's not done until the paperwork is finished'

Documentation is the bugbear of the programmer – until, of course, the programmer has to sort out someone else's program! Commercial organizations usually try to encourage programmers to document their programs well. They tell the old and probably fictitious story about the programmer who had a program 95% complete, did no documentation and then went out and got run over by a bus. The colleagues who remained allegedly had a terrible job trying to continue work on the program.
    Program documentation typically consists of the following ingredients:

- the program specification
- the source code, including appropriate comments
- design information, for example pseudo-code
- the test schedule
- the test results
- the modification history
- the user manual (if needed).

If you ever get asked to take over someone's program, this is what you will need – but don't expect to get it!

Programmers generally find creating documentation a boring chore and tend to skimp on it. They generally leave it to the end of the project, when there's little time available. No wonder it is often not done or done poorly.

The only way to ease the pain is to do the documentation as you go along, mixing it in with the more interesting tasks of programming.

Programming pitfalls

Don't spend hours and hours making your program beautiful only then to find that there is a prettyfier program available. Check what prettyfiers are available *before* you start to code. Also check whether there are any house standards in your organization before you start to code.

Summary

- Program style is important to promote readability for debugging and maintenance.
- Guidelines for good program layout embrace names, indentation, blank lines and comments.
- C++ has a useful facility for making selected data items constant.
- Careful choice of parameters for functions is worth while.
- Functions should not be too long and can be placed together in related groups.
- There are two possible schemes for where to place function prototypes.
- Nested if statements, loops and complex conditions should be used judiciously.
- Good documentation is always worthy.

Bibliography

The following book is a classic old book that refers to FORTRAN and PL/I. But it is equally applicable to C++.

The Elements of Programming Style by BW Kernighan and P J Plauger, McGraw-Hill, Maidenhead, 1978.

The following book describes the results of the experiments that have been carried out to decide which program styles are clearest:

Psychology of Programming edited by Jean-Marie Hoc, Academic Press, London, 1990.

CHAPTER 21

Effective programming

Introduction

Programming is enormous fun. We can all spend happy hours on the computer watching our programs grow. However, in commercial organizations, things can be different. Programmers often have to work to cruel deadlines. There may be all kinds of constraints, like ensuring that the testing is done properly and providing adequate documentation. So it's important to know how to go about programming effectively – even if you the break the rules!

The stages of programming

The classical series of steps in developing a program are:

1 study the specification
2 clarify the specification, if necessary
3 design the program
4 code the program (on paper)
5 key in the program
6 correct the program using the editor
7 compile, link and run
8 debug and test
9 repeat steps 6 to 8 until the testing is satisfactory
10 complete the documentation
11 maintenance.

The specification

Study of the specification is vital so that you know precisely what is required. Specifications often contain ambiguities and omissions and it is therefore often necessary to meet with the person who specified the program to clarify (preferably in writing) what is wanted. We looked at a specification in the chapter on debugging (Chapter 17).

Testing and debugging

It is instructive to realize that professional programmers typically spend half the time on testing and debugging. This gives some idea of how important and how difficult it is. It is rare for a program, however small, to work properly first time. Debugging and testing are discussed in Chapters 17 and 18 respectively.

Piecemeal programming

In Chapter 19 – on piecemeal programming – we explain how the above, strictly step-by-step approach can be relaxed.

Maintenance

Last, but not least, on the list of steps is what is the most time-consuming activity of all – maintenance. Students of programming tend not to do program maintenance, so it can be something of a mystery. Maintenance is what happens after a program has (apparently) been completed and put into use. What happens then is that bugs are revealed as users use the program for real. Soon the users also realize that they would like the program to do additional things or different things. So there are two types of maintenance:

- remedial – correcting bugs
- adaptive – changing the program to meet new user needs.

All together, as much time is often spent on the maintenance of a program as was spent on developing the program in the first place.

Now maintenance is easier if the program was well designed when it was written, and if the documentation is complete and clear. This brings us on to our next topic.

Documentation

The purpose of documentation is to help the user of the program and to help the programmers who are to come afterwards. For the user, documentation includes, at a minimum:

the specification
a user manual.

For the maintenance programmer, documentation includes, at a minimum:

the program listing
the results of testing.

Writing documentation, vital though it is, is not usually regarded as the most fun activity within programming. Therefore the recommendation is to write the documentation of the program little by little throughout the process of development, rather than leave what might be a big, boring job until the end.

The importance of design

Program design is the act of devising the grand-scale structure of a program. We looked at the process of design and one method for design in Chapter 11.

There are a number of approaches to program design. The most notorious approach to design is not to do design at all! This approach is called *hacking*. In hacking, the programmer simply sits down at the keyboard and starts keying in pieces of the program. Development proceeds in a delightfully anarchic manner, with experimentation as a central ingredient.

The trouble is that if you are a novice programmer, it is very difficult to adopt any sort of a systematic approach to programming. It takes time to learn to adopt a careful, systematic approach.

Hacking has a bad press. It is generally thought to be irresponsible, time wasting and liable to lead to a poor end-product. The program will therefore be difficult to test and to maintain.

There's not actually a lot of hard evidence that hacking is unproductive and leads to poor products, but there's a great suspicion that it does. So most people place a lot of emphasis on systematic approaches to programming.

Summary

- There are a number of well-defined steps in programming.
- Effective programming may save time and lead to a better program.
- A disorganized, but thoroughly enjoyable, approach is called hacking.

CHAPTER 22
What next?

Now that you have read and studied this book, what do you know, what can you do and what do you do next?

Hopefully you have written a number of programs, keyed them into your computer, run and tested them.

You can now develop small to medium-sized programs in C++. You know about one approach to program design. You know the problems of testing and how to cope with them.

You should be able to learn C fairly easily. The differences are explained in Appendix F.

You will also be able to learn fairly easily languages which are in the same family as C++, like Ada, Basic, Modula 2, and Pascal. They are fairly similar to C++. COBOL uses the same concepts, but is a large and cumbersome language.

What about object-oriented programming? Well, you will need all you have learned about C++ programming from this book:

variables
assignment
calculation
repetition using while
choice using if
functions.

Then you will need to learn about the additional concepts of classes and objects, inheritance and polymorphism. It's an exciting study and it's the flavour of the decade. See the bibliography for books on the subject.

Answers to self-test questions

1 You and the computer

Question: What is a computer? What is the difference between hardware and software?
Answer: A computer is a machine that obeys instructions within a program.
   Hardware is the boxes and circuitry of the computer. You can touch and see it. Software is the collection of programs that runs on a computer.

Question: What does an operating system do?
Answer: It allows the user to communicate with the computer using the keyboard and mouse. It provides facilities to run programs.

Question: What does a filing system do?
Answer: A filing system provides the facility to store information on a disk in the form of files.

Question: What does an editor do?
Answer: It provides facilities to change the contents of a file on disk or else to create an entirely new file.

Question: List and explain the steps involved in preparing a program to run on a computer.
Answer:
1   Using the editor, key in, correct and store the program in a file on disk.
2   Compile the program – convert it to machine code.
3   Link the program with any library programs that are used by the program using the linker.
4   Load the program into memory and run it.

Question: What is a computer program?
Answer: A computer program is a series of instructions for a computer to obey. The instructions can direct the computer to carry out a sequence of actions, a choice of actions (following a test) and/or a repeated series of actions.

2 Data and actions

Question: What is wrong with this?

```
cin << alice:
```

Answer: The arrows point the wrong way.

Question: Which of these potential names are valid and which are invalid. Why?

running_total, main, 1st_value, SUM, again, Salary_for_1999, cost-code

Answer: The following are valid:

running_total, SUM, again, Salary_for_1999

The following are invalid:

main (it is a special word), 1st_value (it starts with a digit), cost-code (has a hyphen)

Question: Carefully check what the following program extract achieves:

```
int Alice, Tom;

cin >> Alice >> Tom;

Alice = Tom;
Tom = Alice;

cout << Alice << Tom;
```

Answer: Although it might look as if the program fragment should interchange the two values, it fails to do so. Alice is first given the value of Tom. But now the original value of Alice has been lost. The final step only serves to make Tom equal to its original value.

Question: Now look at the following piece of program and convince yourself that it successfully interchanges the values:

```
int Alice, Tom, Save;

cin >> Alice >> Tom;

Save = Alice;
Alice = Tom;
```

```
Tom = Save;

cout << Alice << Tom;
```

Answer: One way to do this is to use paper and pencil, writing down and changing the values of the variables Alice, Save and Tom as the program executes.

Question: What does this piece of program do?

```
int year_of_birth, year_is_21;

cin >> year_of_birth;
year_is_21 = year_of_birth + 21;
cout << year_is_21;
```

Answer: The program inputs a value into the variable year_of_birth. It adds 21 to that value and places the answer in the variable year_is_21. This value is then output.

Overall, the program inputs a year of birth and calculates the year when the person will be 21.

Question: What does this piece of program do?

```
int wage, tax, pay;

cin >> wage >> tax;
pay = wage - tax;
cout << pay;
```

Answer: The program inputs values for a wage and a tax. It outputs the pay, which is equal to the wage minus the tax.

Question: What does this sequence do?

```
char this_one, that_one;

cin >> this_one;
that_one=this_one;
cout << that_one;
this_one = '?';
cout << this_one;
```

Answer: The program inputs a single character, and then places a copy in the variable that_one. This value is output. Next a question mark is placed in the variable this_one and output.

The overall effect is to input a character and echo it on the screen, followed by a question mark.

Question: What is the effect of this statement?

```
// cout << "Don't forget to save your file";
```

Answer: None, because the statement is treated as a comment.

3 Decisions – if

Question: Do these two pieces of C++ coding achieve the same end or not?

```
if (age > 18) cout << "you can vote";
if (age < 18) cout << "you cannot vote";
```

Answer: No. The first statement says that you can vote if you are over 18 – that is, 19 or more. The second statement says that you cannot vote if you are less than 18 – that is, 17 or younger. The question of what happens if you are exactly 18 years old is treated differently in the two tests.

Question: Write if statements to test whether someone should get a pension. The rules are:

You get a pension if you are a man and over 65
If you are a woman you get a pension at age 60

Answer:
if (you are a man and your age > 65) you get a pension
if (you are a woman and your age > 60) you get a pension

Question: Re-write the if statement given in the text without using the not operator.
Answer:

```
if (age < = 18)
    cout << "too young";
```

Question: Write C++ code to input a salary and determine how much tax someone should pay according to the following rules:

People pay no tax if they earn less than £6000. They pay tax at the rate of 20% on the amount they earn over £5000 but less than £20,000. They pay tax at 90% on any money they earn over £20,000

Answer:

```
int salary, tax;

cin >> salary;
tax=0;
if (salary > 5000 && salary < 20000) tax = (salary-5000)*0.2;
if (salary > 20000) tax = (salary-20000)*0.9 + (15000*0.2);
cout << tax;
```

4 Repetition – while and for

Question: What would this program fragment do?

```
int counter;
counter = 0;
while (counter < = 8)
    {
    cout << "*";
    counter ++;
    }
```

Answer: Output nine asterisks. The loop repeats for counter equal to 0, and then in steps of 1 up to counter equal to 8.

Question: Alter the program in the text slightly so that it inputs integer numbers and adds them together until a negative number is input. The negative number is not part of the total.
Answer:

```
sum=0;
cin >> number;

while (number > = 0)
    {
    sum = sum + number;
    cin >> number;
    }
cout << sum;
```

Question: Write a program that uses a for statement to input and add together 10 numbers that are input from the keyboard.

Answer:

```
int count, number, total;
total=0;
for (count=0; count < 10; count ++)
    {
    cin >> number;
    total=total+number;
    }
```

Question: Re-write the `for` loop given in the text to output asterisks using a `while` statement instead.
Answer:

```
number_required=8;
count = 0
while (count < number_required)
    {
    cout << "*";
    cout << endl;
    count++;
    }
```

Question: Write a program to input numbers from the keyboard and add them together. The sequence of numbers ends either with the number 0 or the number 999.
Answer:

```
int number, total;

total=0;
cin >> number;
while (! ((number=0) || (number=999)))
    {
    total=total+number;
    cin >> number;
    }
```

5 Calculations

Question: What do these mean?

```
2+3+4 // 9

2-3+4 // left to right, gives 3

2*3/4 // gives 6/4, which gives 1 because they are integers

2/3*4 // the division is done first, giving 1. This is
  multiplied by 4 giving 4.

a * b + c - d/3 // multiply a by b giving x
                // divide d by e giving y
                // now do x + c - y, left to right
```

6 Character data

Question: Write a fragment of program that inputs a date in the format:

28/12/2005

so that the three numbers are input into three integer variables called day, month and year.
Answer:

```
int day, month, year;
char separator;

cin >> day;
cin >> separator;
cin >> month;
cin >> separator;
cin >> year;
```

Question: Write a fragment of program to test whether a particular character is a vowel or not.
Answer:

```
char c;

if (c == 'a' || c =='e' || c == 'i' || c == 'o' || c == 'u')
    cout << c << "is a vowel";
```

7 Functions

Question: A program is about to be written and it has been recognized that there is a need to output a line of dashes to the screen several times during the execution of the program. Write a function to provide such a service. Give the function the name Dashes.
Answer:

```
void Dashes (void)
{
cout << "— — — — — — — — — — — — — — — — — — — — — — — — — — ";
}
```

Question: Which of these are valid function names?

add, convert_to_integer, Input_Data, main, function_2

Answer: All except main, which is reserved for the name of the main function in any program.

Question: Write the prototype for the function Dashes that was the subject of an earlier question.
Answer:

```
void Dashes (void);
```

Question: Write a function called male to fit in with the program given in the text and display some information about your favourite male artist.
Answer:

```
void male (void)
{
cout << "the best male performer is";
cout << "Bruce Springsteen";
};
```

You might disagree with the performer, but you should have a program structure like this one!

Question: Write prototypes for the functions given in the text.
Answer:

```
void new_artist (void);
void old_artist (void);
```

```
void female (void);
void male (void);
```

8 Functions with parameters

Question: Write a program that uses the function line, given in the text, to output the following pattern:

```
*
**
***
****
```

Answer:

```
line (1);
line (2);
line (3);
line (4);
```

Question: Write a program that uses the function line, given in the text, to output the following pattern:

```
*
**
* ∧ ∧
****
```

Answer:

```
line ('*',1);
line ('*',2);
line ('*',3);
line ('*',4);
```

Question: What is the effect of writing this call on the function line, given in the text?

```
line (22, '+');
```

Answer: This is erroneous, because the parameters are in the wrong order. The compiler will give an error message.

Question: Write a program that input two integers, uses the function `larger` (given in the text) and outputs the result obtained by the function.
Answer:

```
int num1, num2, bigger;

cin >> num1;
cin >> num2;
larger (num1, num2, bigger);
cout << bigger;
```

Question: Write a function that adds one to the value of its parameter (an integer).
Answer:

```
void add_one (int & number)
{
    number++;
}
```

Question: Write a function that converts a time measured in minutes and seconds into the same time measured in seconds.
Answer:

```
void convert (int mins, int secs, int & total_secs)
{
    total_secs=secs + (mins*60);
}
```

Question: Explain why functions are useful in programming.
Answer: They enable (potentially) large and complex programs to be constructed from small, manageable components.

9 Functions that return values

Question: Write a function called add_one that adds one to the value of an integer that is supplied to the function as a parameter. Write the function in two different ways – once returning the value as a parameter and once returning the value as the value of the function (using `return`).
Answer:

```
void add_one (int number, int & new_number)
{
    new_number=number+1;
```

```
    }

    int add_one (int number)
    {
        return (number+1);
    }
```

Question: Given below are the partial specifications of a number of functions. For each function:

1 decide on a name for the function
2 think about how the function would be used
3 decide which items should be parameters
4 decide what (if any) should be returned as the value of the function
5 write the prototype for each function (but do not write the function itself).

The outline descriptions of the functions are:

1 calculate the area of a triangle from a height and base
2 convert a time measured in seconds into hours, minutes and seconds
3 convert a time measured in hours, minutes and seconds into seconds
4 put three characters into alphabetical order
5 given two characters, return the first one (in alphabetical order).

Answers:

```
1   float area_of_triangle (float height, float base);
2   void convert_from_secs (int secs, int & hours, int & mins, int &
    new_secs);
3   int convert_to_secs (int hours, int mins, int secs);
4   void order (char & x, char & y, char & z);
5   char first (char one_char, char another_char);
```

Question: Write the prototype for the alternative version of function Human_Go.
Answer:

```
    char Human_Go (void);
```

Question: Re-write function Computer_Go so as to use a return value, rather than a parameter.
Answer:

```
    char Computer_Go (void)
    {
        int random_number;
        void display_choice (char);
```

```
    random_number=rand() % 3;

    if (random_number==0) choice='r';
    if (random_number==1) choice='s';
    if (random_number==2) choice='p';

    cout << "The computer chose";
    display_choice (choice);
    return (choice);
}
```

10 Global data

11 Program design

12 Arrays

Question: Declare an array to hold figures for the rain that falls each day for a week.
Answer:

```
int rain[7];
```

Question: Given the declaration:

```
int table[2];
```

how long is the array and what is the valid range of subscripts?
Answer: The length is 2. The valid subscripts are 0 and 1.

Question: What would this do?

```
int sale[7], sum;
int day;

sum=0;
for (day=0; day <=7; day++)
{
```

```
    sum=sum+sale[day];
}
```

Answer: Accumulates the sum of all of the elements in the array called sale. (There are seven elements in the array.) Then it adds to the total whatever is in computer memory immediately after the array. This is almost certainly not what the programmer intended!

Question: Write a function that displays an array of characters on the screen. The parameters of the function are the array and its length.
Answer:

```
void display (char array[], int length)
{
    int s;

    for (s=0; s<length; s++)
        cout << array[s];
}
```

Question: Write a function that inputs the values of an array of integers. The parameters for the function are the array and its length.
Answer:

```
void input(int array[], int length)
{
    int s;
    for (s=0; s<length; s++)
        cin >> array[s];
}
```

Question: Alter the piece of program (given in the text) to find the largest item in an array so that it also finds the position (subscript number) of the largest element.
Answer:

```
int table[10];
int largest, i;
int position;

largest = table[0];
position=0;

for (i=0; i<10; i++)
    if (table[i] > largest)
```

```
        {
        largest = table[i];
        position = i;
        }
```

Question: In the program fragment given in the text, the condition in the `while` loop is quite complicated. can it be written differently? Does the following condition perform the same task?

```
while (!((c='.') || (s=20)) )
```

Answer: Yes, it can be written differently. Yes, the suggested code has the same effect.

Question: A program is to store and manipulate rainfall figures for each day of the week. An array is to be used to store the seven values. Write C++ statements to declare the array and to fill it with zeros. Make use of `const` as appropriate.
Answer:

```
const int days=7;
float rainfall[days] = {0};
```

Question: Declare an array of 100 characters and fill it with the letter x as part of the declaration.
Answer:

```
const int size=100;
char array_of_chars[size] = {'x'};
```

13 Arrays – two dimensional

Question: Declare an array to represent a chess board. A chess board is eight squares by eight squares. Each position in the array should hold a single character.
Answer:

```
char chess_board[8][8];
```

Question: Write C++ statements to place a space character on every square of an 8 by 8 chess board that is represented as a two-dimensional array of characters.
Answer:

```
int row, col;
```

```
for (row=0; row<8; row++)
     for (col=0; col<8; col++)
          chess_board[row][col]=' ';
```

Question: Write a C++ function to place a space character on every square of an 8 by 8 chess board that is represented as a two-dimensional array of characters. Try to make the function as general as possible. For example, the name of the array should ideally be a parameter. It is possible to make the size of the array a parameter?
Answer:

```
void fill_spaces(char table[][8], row_size);
{
     int row, col;
     int const col_size=8;

     for (row=0; row<row_size; row++)
          for (col+0; col<col_size; col++)
               table[row][col]=' ';
}
```

It is possible to make the second dimension of the array a parameter, but not the first.

Question: Re-write the sample operations on arrays given in the text to

input values
multiply each element by itself
output the values

as functions that are as general purpose as possible.
Answer:

```
void input (int table[][5], int row_size);
{
     int row, col;

     for (row=0; row<row_size; row++)
          for (col=0; col<5; col++)
               cin >> table[row][col];
}


void input (int table[][5], int row_size);
{
     int row, col;
```

```
    for (row=0; row<row_size; row++)
        for (col=0; col<5; col++)
            table[row][col] = table[row][col]*
              table[row][col];
}


void input (int table[][5], int row_size);
{
    int row, col;

    for (row=0; row<row_size; row++)
        for (col=0; col<5; col++)
            cout << table[row][col];
}
```

Question: Write the declaration of a 10 by 10 array of characters in such a way that the array is filled with spaces.
Answer:

```
char table[10][10] = {' '};
```

14 Pointers

Question: Draw a diagram to illustrate what has happened to the variables Ben, x and p in the program fragment given in the text.
Answer:

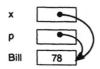

Question: Work out what this program extract does:

```
int i,j;
int *p1, *p2;

i = 66;
p1 = &i;
```

```
p2 = p1;
j = *p2;
```

Answer: (as comments alongside):

```
int i, j;          // declare two integers
int * p1, * p2;    // declare two pointers to integers

i = 66;            // integer i becomes 66
p2 = &i;           // pointer p1 becomes a pointer to integer i
p2 = p1;           // pointer p2 becomes equal to the value of
                   // pointer p1
                   // (which points to i)
j = *p2;           // integer j becomes equal to the integer
                   // pointed to by pointer p2.
                   // Since p2 points to i, and i contains the
                   // value 66,
                   // j becomes equal to i which is 66
```

15 Strings

Question: A date in the form:

28 June 2015

is to be input into the computer. There is a space between each of the items in the date. Write C++ statements to input the three components of a date into three distinct string variables.

Answer:

```
int day;
char month[20];
int year;

cin >> day;
cin >> month;
cin >> year;
```

Question: Write a piece of program that inputs a name from the keyboard and compares it with the name 'Charles'. If the name is the same, the program outputs 'You are famous'. Otherwise it outputs 'You are a nerd'.

Answer:

```
char name[25];

cin >> name;
if (strcmp(name, "Charles") == 0)
    cout << "You are famous";
else
    cout << "You are a nerd";
```

Question: Write a program that inputs any name from the keyboard and displays how long the name is.
Answer:

```
char name[25];

cin >> name;
cout << strlen(name);
```

Question: Write the code in the text to extract the job title of the person from the record.
Answer: This requires only a small addition to the existing code. Two initial searches for a colon will take us to the start of the job description information. So adding an additional call to the string search function will do the job:

```
// the information about the person
char personal_details[]=
  "Mike Bower: 7.5.68:programmer:40000";
// a pointer ready to point to the start of the job field
char *begin[];
// a pointer ready to point to the end of the job field
char *end[];
// a string ready to hold the job information
char job[20];

// search the string for a colon character at the start of
    the date of birth
begin = strchr (personal_details, ':');
// increment the pointer past the colon
begin ++;
// search again for the colon at the start of the job
    description
begin = strchr (begin, ':');
// increment the pointer past the colon
```

```
begin++;
// search the string again for a colon character
end = strchr (begin, ':');
// place NUL at the end of the job field
*end = NUL;
// copy the job information out of the original string
strcpy (job, begin);
// output the required information
cout << "The job is" << job;
```

16 File processing

Question: Devise a line of data for the file described in the text.
Answer:

12 6 97 h 4 3

Question: Create a small file of the football information using your text editor. Then run the program in the text and verify that it reads and displays the information correctly.
Answer: Use your text editor to create a file of suitable data. Some illustrative data is given in the text. It must end with the line:

99 99 99 h 0 0

to make the end of the file.

The program should display the data that you put into the file, but not including the terminating line.

Question: Run the program in the text in order to create a new file. Make sure that you do not destroy any file that you have already created, because creating a file will obliterate any information that was in the file beforehand. Check that it has been created correctly by examining it with your text editor.
Answer: Use lines of data that conform to the same layout (day month year home or away score). End the data with a line like this:

99 99 99 h 0 0

The program should end. Use your text editor to inspect the contents of the file that you should have created.

Question: Run the program given in the text. When this works correctly, you may find that you wish to delete the special end of file line with the meaningless day value of 99.

Question: Again, run the program given in the text and check that it has correctly appended a new line of information to the end of the file by examining the lengthened file using your text editor.

Answer: Your program should display whatever data you have put in the file. (If in doubt about the contents of a file, use the text editor to inspect its contents.)

Question: Given two differences between arrays and serial files.

Answer:

1   An array is held in main memory. A file is held on disk.
2   An array element is accessed by means of a subscript. An item in a file is accessed by reading data (starting at the beginning of the file) until the required item is reached.

(Once created, both a file and an array are of fixed length and can't be changed.)

17 Debugging

Question: What is the difference between debugging and testing?

Answer: Testing reveals the existence of a bug – somewhere. Debugging finds where the bug is and eliminates it.

18 Testing

Question: A program's function is to input three integer numbers and find the largest. Devise black box test data for this program.

Answer: We need clearer information in order to test this program properly. For example, are the numbers positive and negative? Let us assume that the numbers are all in the range $-32,768$ to $+32,767$.

Let us choose some representative numbers:

    8   9   10

We might argue that any integer is representative of all the others, so that these values are typical of all other data values.

There are several cases, tested with data as follows:

    8   9   10
    8   10   9
    10   9   8

    10   10   10   (all three the same)
    10   10   8   (two the same)

If we were now worried that we were not properly testing the range of numbers, we could use:

  −32,768   32,767   0

in various combinations.

Question: In a program to play the game of chess, the player specifies the destination for a move as a pair of subscripts, the row and column number. The program checks that the destination square is valid – that is, not outside the board. Devise black box test data to check that this part of the program is working correctly.

Answer: Let us assume that valid subscripts are the numbers in the range 1 to 8.

We need to use as test data both numbers in the range and numbers outside the range. We could argue that numbers on the boundary of the range need to be tested, because they are a 'sensitive' region. So we suggest the following test data:

  1, 1   (near the boundary)
  1, 8
  8, 1
  0, 0   (near the boundary)
  9, 9   (near the boundary)

Question: A program's function is to input three numbers and find the largest. Devise white box test data for this program.

The code is:

```
int a, b, c;

cin >> a >> b >> c;

if (a > b)
    if (a > c) cout << a
        else cout << c;
else
    if (b > c) cout << b
        else cout << c;
```

Answer: There are four paths through the program, one for each cout statement. Therefore we choose four sets of test data, one for each path:

  10   9   8
  10   9   11
  8   9   7
  8   9   10

Question: In a program to play the game of chess, the player specifies the destination for a move as a pair of subscripts, the row and column number. The program checks that the destination square is valid – that is, not outside the board. Devise white box test data to check that this part of the program is working correctly.

The code for this part of the program is:

```
into row, col;

cin >> row >> col;

if ((row > 8) || (row < 1)) cout << "error";
if ((col > 8) || (col < 1)) cout << "error";
```

Answer: Two paths lead to the output of the error message and one path leads to no error message. But each if statement has within it two conditions. Therefore there are implicitly two paths within each if. Overall, there are five paths with illustrative data as follows:

```
9   5
-1  5
5   9
5  -1
4   4
```

19 Piecemeal programming

20 Program style

Question: Enhance the coding to draw the block of flats so that the number of floors and the number of flats on each floor are both variables. Pass as parameters the number of flats per floor and the number of floors.
Answer:

```
void draw_block (int no_of_floors, int flats_per_floor)
{
    int floor;

    for (floor=0; floor < no_of_floors; floor++)
        {
        draw_floor(flats_per_floor);
        cout << endl;
        }
}
```

```
void draw_floor(int no_of_flats)
{
    int flat;

    for (flat=0; flat < no_of_flats; flat++)
        cout << "F";
}
```

Annotated bibliography

.

This appendix names selected books that would be useful for further reading and makes comments about each book.

C++

If you want to know more about C++, there is a large number of books. Be warned, some of them are very weighty and formidable! The simplest of the lot, and the one that seems to follow on very well from this text is:

Problem Solving, Abstraction, and Design using C++ by Frank L Friedman and Elliot B Koffman, Addison-Wesley, Reading, MA, 1994.

Another, readable, text is:

Instant C++ Programming by Ian Wilks, WROX Press, Birmingham, 1994.

which is not at all silly, as its title might imply.

One book bravely plunges in by starting with object-oriented concepts from the very start. This would be a good book to look at once you are happy with the basic ideas of programming.

The Object Concept. An Introduction to Computer Programming Using C++ by Rick Decker and Stuart Hirshfield, International Thomson, London, 1995.

There is a large number of weighty and comprehensive books on C++. Examples are:

C++ How to Program by H M Deitel and P J Deitel, Prentice Hall, Englewood Cliffs, NJ, 1994.
C++ Complete: A Reference and Tutorial to the Proposed C++ Standard by Anthony Rudd, John Wiley, Chichester, 1995.
C++ Problem Solving and Programming by Kenneth A Barclay and Brian J Gordon, Prentice Hall, Englewood Cliffs, NJ, 1993.

The 'bible' of C++ is:

The C++ Programming Language by B Stroustrup, 2nd edn, Addison-Wesley, Reading, MA, 1986.

This really is an epic book, written by the inventor of C++. It is long, comprehensive, rich – but you could spend a lifetime studying it. It is definitely *not* recommended for the novice. Instead it is to be recommended for someone who is very experienced in programming.

Another really formidable book is what is currently regarded as the book describing 'standard' C++:

The Annotated C++ Reference Manual by Margaret A Ellis and Bjarne Stroustrup, Addison-Wesley, Reading, MA, 1990.

Object-oriented programming

If you want to know about the principles of object-oriented programming and about object-oriented design, then the 'bible' is:

Object-Oriented Analysis and Design by Grady Booch, Benjamin/Cummings, Redwood City, CA, 1994.

Again, it is not for the faint hearted. You really need to have some experience of programming to understand it. This is a best-selling book and new editions come out fairly frequently. Make sure you get the latest edition.

A very readable book that uses a variety of approaches and notations (including pseudo-code) to object-oriented programming is:

Object-Oriented Software Engineering with C++ by Darrel Ince, McGraw-Hill, Maidenhead, 1991.

Other programming languages

A gentle introduction to the language Pascal is:

Pascal Simply by Doug Bell and Peter Scott, Chartwell-Bratt, Bromley, Kent, 1994.

and a similar book on C is:

C Simply by Mike Parr, Chartwell-Bratt, Bromley, Kent, 1994.

Yet another in this series of simple books is one on the language Ada:

Ada Simply by Mike Parr, Chartwell-Bratt, Bromley, Kent, 1993.

Programming in general

A whole series of books seek to describe programs without concentrating too much on a particular programming language. Perhaps the best of these is:

Programming Classics. Implementing the World's Best Algorithms by Ian Oliver, Prentice Hall, Hemel Hempstead, 1993.

This presents, as its title says, a collection of classic programs from a variety of applications. The programs are given in pseudo-code and in a clear hybrid programming language, which users of C++ should find easy.

Another such book is:

Problems in Programming – Experience through Practice by Andrej Vitek *et al.*, John Wiley, Chichester, 1991.

The first chapter is on the principles of good programming. Subsequent chapters explore the development of a series of interesting programs. The programming language is Pascal.

Another book that presents a comprehensive list of important programs is:

Algorithms by Robert Sedgewick, Addison-Wesley, Reading, MA, 1988.

The programming language used is, again, Pascal. This is not a book for the novice – for example, some of the programs deal with exotic data structures, like graphs and trees. It's really something of a compendium of useful programs, for reference should it be needed.

There's a book which, as its title suggests, tries to present common programs:

Common Algorithms in Pascal with Programs for Reading by David V Moffat, Prentice Hall, Englewood Cliffs, NJ, 1984.

The problem with the book is that very little use is made of the Pascal equivalent of functions (procedures), so that the programs tend to look long and complicated. But reading other people's programs can be very instructive – even if they are not very good!

Program style

There's one classic book that looks at style:

Elements of Programming Style by Brian W Kernighan and P J Plauger, 2nd edn, McGraw-Hill, Maidenhead, 1978.

It's an oldie, but a goodie. The examples are given in FORTRAN and PL/I, but the lessons are relevant to C++. It's very readable and full of good advice.

A slightly younger book concentrates on the language C:

C Programming Standards and Guidelines by Thomas Plum, 2nd edn, Plum Hall, Kamuela, HI, NJ, 1981.

The most recent book is the following, which again is about C, rather than C++. It is most readable.

C Style: Standards and Guidelines by David Straker, Prentice Hall, Englewood Cliffs, NJ, 1992.

Program design

A book that surveys various approaches to program design is:

Program Design by Doug Bell, Ian Morrey and John Pugh, Prentice Hall, Hemel Hempstead, 1996.

The book:

Programming on Purpose. Essays on Software Design by P J Plauger, Prentice Hall, Englewood Cliffs, NJ, 1993.

is a wonderfully readable collection of essays. The author argues for having a variety of design approaches, each applicable to some range of problems.

The following book presents one approach to program design called data structure design, Jackson structured programming or JSP. It is described in:

Principles of Program Design by Michael A. Jackson, Academic Press, London, 1975.

The psychology of programming

Some people have looked at programming from a psychological point of view. It makes fascinating reading. They describe how people actually think when they go about programming. They assess what makes programs clear to read and understand. Here are the major books taking this perspective (the first is an oldie, but a goodie):

The Psychology of Computer Programming by Gerald Weinberg, 1971.
Software Psychology by Ben Shneiderman, Winthrop, Cambridge, MA, 1980.
Psychology of Programming edited by Jean-Marie Hoc, *et al.* Academic Press, London, 1990.

Artificial life (a-life)

We have used some small examples from the field of artificial life in this book. A most enjoyable discussion of a-life is:

Artificial Life. The Quest for a New Creation by Steven Levy, Penguin Books, Harmondsworth, 1993.

Programmers – their lives and work

There have been a few exciting accounts of the personal outlook and work methods of programmers. They give insights into how programming is actually done. They also contribute to the folklore of programming.

An example of such a book is:

Programmers at Work by Susan Lammers, Microsoft, Redmond, WA, 1986.

In the book, she reports on interviews with notable programmers.
Another really exciting book is:

Hackers. Heroes of the Computer Revolution by Steven Levy, Anchor Books, Peterborough,
1984.

which charts the lives of the early 'real programmers'.

If you are interested in how software projects really get done and what life is like
at Microsoft, the following book is a good read:

*Show-Stopper. The Breakneck Race to Create Windows NT and the Next Generation at
Microsoft* by G Pasacal Zachary, Free Press, Macmillan, New York, 1994.

Software development

If you would like to know about the problems of (and some of the solutions to)
developing large-scale software, the following is very readable:

Software Development: Fashioning the Baroque by Darrel Ince, Oxford University Press,
Oxford, 1988.

Life within Microsoft and the lessons that can be learned are well presented in:

Debugging the Development Process by Steve Maguire, Microsoft, Redmond, WA, 1994.

This book has the subtitle *Practical Strategies for Staying Focused, Hitting Ship
Dates and Building Solid Teams*.

Software engineering is the term given to the job of developing large programs.
The following book describes approaches to this task, taking as the reader's starting
point some knowledge of programming:

Software Engineering: A Programming Approach by Doug Bell, Ian Morrey and John Pugh,
Prentice Hall, Hemel Hemsptead, 1987.

Ed Yourdon is one of the gurus of software development. In the book below he
gives a very readable account of the problems that he perceives with software
development today. The book continues by giving a survey of the possible remedies
for the problems. It's altogether a very readable book, free of technicalities and free
with opinions. The title reflects the author's opinion that American programmers
are under threat from competition from programmers in Asia – who are paid less,
but are better!

Decline and Fall of the American Programmer by Edward Yourdon, PTR Prentice Hall,
Englewood Cliffs, NJ, 1993.

Selected C++ libraries

This appendix describes some of the libraries that are available with C++ systems. The libraries described are those that are used in this book. They provide commonly used facilities for performing input, output, calculations, obtaining random numbers and file handling.

Most of these libraries derive from those commonly found with the older language C. There is yet to be any standardization of C++ libraries, and so unfortunately there are sometimes differences between them.

Warning!

Check the manual for your C++ system. Make sure that your system provides these particular functions and that they behave as described in this book.

Input and output

These functions are (almost) standard C++. You can assume that they are available and that they work as described in this book. To use them, you must include:

```
#include <iostream.h>
```

The functions are:

```
cin     input from the keyboard
cout    output to the screen
```

The maths library

To use the following functions, the maths library header must be included like this:

```
#include <math.h>
```

The parameters to these functions must be floating point numbers.

cos (x)	cosine of the angle x, expressed in radians
sin (x)	sine of the angle x, expressed in radians
tan (x)	tangent of the angle x, expressed in radians
fabs (x)	the absolute value of x, sometimes written $|x|$
log (x)	natural logarithm of x (to the base e)
log10 (x)	logarithm of x to base 10
sqrt (x)	the positive square root of x
pow (x, y)	x raised to the power of y, x^y

Random numbers

To use the random number function, you must:

```
#include <stdlib.h>
```

Different systems provide different random number functions. One such function is:

rand   returns a random number in the range 0 to RAND_MAX (usually 32767)

String handling

These functions are in a library and to use one of the functions you must include this statement at the head of your program:

```
#include <string.h>
```

The functions are:

strcpy (to, from)
Copies the string from to the string to, including the terminator, NUL.

strncpy (to, from, n)
Copies at most n characters of string from to string to. If there is room, inserts the terminator, NUL.

strcat (old, new)
Concatenates string new to the end of string old. Adds the terminator at the end.

strncat (old, new, n)
Concatenates at most n characters of string new to the end of string old. Adds the terminator at the end.

`strcmp` (this, that)
Compares string this with string that. Returns zero if they are equal.
If this < that, returns an integer < 0.
If this > that, returns an integer > 0.

`strncmp` (this, that, *n*)
Compares at most *n* characters of string this with string that.
Returns as with `strcmp`.

`strchr` (string, c)
Returns a pointer to the *first* occurrence of character c in the string.
Returns NUL if the character is not in the string.

`strrchr` (string, c)
Returns a pointer to the *last* occurrence of character c in the string.
Returns NUL if the character is not in the string.

`strstr` (string, s)
Returns a pointer to the *first* occurrence of string s in the string.
Returns NUL if s is not in the string.

`strlen` (string)
Returns the length of string, not including the terminator, NUL.

File handling

To use these functions, you need:

```
#include <fstream.h>
```

The functions are:

```
ifstream, ofstream, cin, cout, close
```

and Chapter 16 describes how to use them.

Graphics

There are many useful functions in libraries that draw graphical objects. Unfortunately, this is the area where there is currently the greatest profusion of variety. In this book we have not attempted to look at graphics, simply because there are so many different libraries of graphics functions associated with different systems.

Random numbers

Introduction

If you want to write any kind of computer game program — and you probably will — you will need random numbers. Randomness will ensure that the nasty monsters appear at random places on the screen, rather than at the same boring, predictable position. In any game of chance — say any card game — random numbers are needed. This appendix is about how to do this.

C++ provides a convenient way of getting hold of random numbers, as we will see. To use the facility, we have to include the library stdlib in the usual way:

```
#include <stdlib.h>
```

The random number function

The random number function is called rand, held in the library stdlib that accompanies any C++ system.

To get hold of a random number, you have to call the function rand. The function supplies numbers in the range 0 up to a maximum value called RAND_MAX. This constant, defined in the header file <stlib.h>, is usually 32,767, or 2 to the power 15 minus 1. We call the function like this:

```
ran = rand ();
```

We will not usually want a random number in the range 0 to 32,767. Suppose, for example, we need random numbers in the range 0 to 10 for some purpose. Now one of the special properties of random numbers is that, whatever you do to them, they stay random. So we take the values supplied by the random number generator and convert them. The usual way to do this is to use the remainder operator, %. Remember:

```
a % b
```

gives the remainder after dividing a by b. Therefore, to get a random number in the range 0 to 10 we do the calculation:

```
rand() % 11
```

An example

Suppose we want to deal eight playing cards at random. We are only interested in the value of the cards, not their suit. So we want eight random numbers, each in the range 1 to 13. An ace is 1, a jack is 11 and so on.

Now the random number generator supplies numbers from zero upwards, whereas we want them from 1 upwards. So we'll get random numbers in the range 0 to 12 and then add one to them like this:

```
int count;

for ( count = 1; count <= 8; count++)
    cout << (rand () % 13) + 1;
```

Getting really random numbers

Unless you do something special, the random number generator will always produce the same sequence of (apparently) random numbers every time you run a program that uses it. So, the first time you run a program, it will give the sequence:

867, 45, 3456, 16,934, etc.

and the second time it will give:

867, 45, 3456, 16,934, etc.

This is too predictable and boring. It happens because of the way the random number generator works. The random number generator always starts with a first number, called the seed. It gets the first random number by performing a calculation on the seed that gives an (apparently random) number. It gets the next random number by performing a calculation on the previous number, giving a new (apparently random) number. And so on.

Left to itself, the random number generator starts with the number 1 as the seed. If you want a different series of numbers every time you run a program (and you probably will if you are running a game), you have to give the generator a different seed. To alter it, you call the library function srand, giving as a parameter your value for the seed. For example:

```
srand(42);
```

gives the random number generator the number 42 to use as its seed in creating a series of random numbers.

This isn't much better than leaving the generator to use its own seed, because the generator will again produce the same sequence, but now starting from 42. There are two ways of avoiding the repetition – ask the user for a number or use the clock.

The code to ask the user for a number might look like this:

```
cout << "Give me a starter number for the random numbers";
cin >> seed;
srand(seed);
```

Another approach is to use the clock inside the computer. Now the time expressed in hours is hardly random. The time expressed in minutes is a bit better, but not much. But the seconds part of the current time does look random. It is a number between 0 and 59. So, if we can obtain this figure, we can use it as the seed for the random number generator. Most C++ systems have a library function that provides the time. You will need to look at the documentation for your system to see precisely how to do this, because there is unfortunately no standardization here.

The rules for names in C++

Here are the rules for giving names to data items (variables) and functions in C++.

A name can consist of any number of letters, digits and underlines, but a name must start with a letter.

Upper and lower case letters are distinct, so that, for example, count and Count are two different names.

Some names are reserved by the C++ language for its own use. The programmer cannot use any of them as names. If you do use one of these names, you will get strange error messages from the compiler. The reserved words are:

asm	delete	if	return	try
auto	do	inline	short	typedef
break	double	int	signed	union
case	else	long	sizeof	unsigned
catch	enum	new	static	virtual
char	extern	operator	struct	void
class	float	private	switch	volatile
const	for	protected	template	while
continue	friend	public	this	
default	goto	register	throw	

The above list of names is the 'standard' list of words that are reserved for use by C++. You should check the manual for the C++ system that you are using to see the list that applies.

Some C++ systems may restrict the length of a name. Check the manual for your particular C++ system.

Selected operators – summary

Introduction

This appendix brings together a list of all the C++ operators described in this book. C++ has more than 50 operators. In this book we have chosen to introduce only some of the C++ operators – only 17, in fact. We have selected a wide range of operators, but it is not complete. The reason is simple – they are not all needed. The operators described are a comprehensive range and will enable anyone to write (almost) any kind of program to do exactly what they want. So we have described only those that are necessary to carry out a huge range of programming tasks. You will find the complete set of operators described in more detail in one of the more advanced books on C++ referenced in the annotated bibliography.

The operators used in this book are grouped under headings and at the end we give the flavour of the remainder of the C++ operators.

Comparison operators

These operators compare two integers, two floating point numbers or two characters.

>	means greater than
<	means less than
==	means equals
!=	means not equal to
<=	means less than or equal to
>=	means greater than or equal to

The odd one out in this list is the test for equality, which consists of *two* equals signs, rather than one. It is a common mistake to use just one equals sign in a test.

When used with character data, the comparison operators have the following meanings:

x > y means x comes alphabetically after y
x < y means x comes alphabetically before y

Logical operators

&&   means and
| | means or
!   means not

Arithmetic operators – integers

These operators perform calculations on integers.

+   means add
—   means subtract
*   means multiply
/   means divide and give the quotient (truncated)
%   means divide and give the remainder

Arithmetic operators – floating point numbers

These operators carry out arithmetic on floating point numbers.

+   means add
—   means subtract
*   means multiply
/   means divide

Assignment operators

These operators give a variable a new value.

=   means becomes
++   means increment (add 1 to)
——   means decrement (subtract 1 from)

Pointer operators

&   means pointer to

The other C++ operators

The C++ operators that have not been addressed in this book fall into several groups as follows.

A number of operators support the object-oriented facilities of C++, which are beyond the scope of this book. This is your next challenge, should you choose to accept it.

Some operators provide detailed access to data. If you have some knowledge of how data is stored in a computer, you will know that it is stored in the form of individual binary bits. Each bit is either a 1 or a 0. Bits are grouped into bytes (8 bits) or words (16 or 32 bits). Some of the C++ operators allow access to and manipulation of these individual bits. If you are going to write programs that send and receive data at the level of detail of bits – say data communications or controlling a robot – then you will need to know about this.

Some C++ operators provide shortcuts. We have met two examples of this – the ++ and −− operators. These operators accomplish things that can be done anyway, but do so in an abbreviated way. So that:

    count++;   has the same effect as   count=count+1;

Using shortcuts like this makes a program shorter to write, but arguably sometimes more difficult to understand. It can make the program run more quickly, if this is important in the particular application being programmed. If you intend to become a professional C++ programmer who knows all the details of C++, then you will probably learn about these in due course.

APPENDIX F

C and C++: some differences

This appendix describes the differences between those parts of C++ described in this book and the equivalent in C.

If you have learned C++ from this book, you should have little difficulty in learning C from the information in this appendix.

C and C++ are very similar languages; indeed C++ was developed from C. The relationship is that C is a subset of C++; C++ is a superset of C. Any C program will compile and run under a C++ system. The opposite is not true.

There are two areas of difference – input/output and parameter passing.

Input/output

The C++ statement:

```
cout << x;
```

has the following equivalent in C:

```
printf ("%d", x);
```

The function called printf is the equivalent of cout. The name is short for print formatted and dates back to the time before VDUs when output tended to be to printers. printf is called, as you can see, using the normal grammar for function calling. The string %d, in quotes, specifies the layout of the information to be output – in this case a decimal number.

If we wanted to output the values of two integer variables x and y, we write:

```
printf ("%d%d", x, y);
```

Text is output like this:

```
printf ("hello mum \n");
```

in which the character pair \n means go to a newline – like endl.

If a floating point number is to be output, then the layout must be specified as %f.

It is common to see `printf` statements that combine numbers and text like this:

```
printf ("x is %d and y is %f \n", x,y);
```

Now to input, the C++ statement:

```
cin >> x;
```

has the following equivalent in C:

```
scanf ("%d", &x);
```

The function called `scanf` (short for scan formatted) is the equivalent of `cin`. The string `%d`, in quotes, specifies the layout of the information to be input – in this case a decimal number.

If we wanted to input two numbers into integer variables x and y, we write:

```
scanf ("%d%d", &x, &y);
```

If x is a floating point number and y is integer:

```
scanf ("%d%f", &x, &y);
```

Parameter passing

C++ is different from C in the way that parameters are identified in function calling.

In C++ a parameter whose value is going to be changed by the function is specially marked with an ampersand in the function header (and in the prototype). That is all you have to do.

In C, things are more complicated:

1   In the function header (and prototype), a parameter whose value is going to be changed by the function does *not* need to be identified by an ampersand (&).
2   Within the function, everywhere that a parameter which is to be changed is used, it must be specially marked with an asterisk (*) in front of it. It is easy to forget this asterisk and this is therefore a rich source of errors in C programs.
3   When a function is called, any parameters that are to be changed are specially marked with an ampersand (&). This is another likely source of errors.

Here is an example of a C function:

```
void largest (int x, int y, int larger)
{
if (x > y)
    *larger=x;
else
    *larger=y;
}
```

and a call on this function:

```
largest(a, b, & bigger);
```

Object-oriented programming (OOP)

The greatest differences between C and C++ lie in the area of object-oriented programming (OOP) – a subject beyond the scope of this book.

Briefly, OOP is about grouping together variables and functions that are closely related. These groupings are called objects. A program consists of any number of these objects. Each object is self-contained and the program is consequently very modular.

It is also argued that it is very natural to represent the structure of a problem being solved by mimicking the objects that are in the problem by objects within the program.

Sample program – rock, scissors, paper

This appendix contains the text of a complete C++ program. A description of the development of the program is given in Chapter 9.

The specification of the program is:

As played by humans, the game is as follows. Two people face each other, with one hand behind their backs. On a signal, both reveal their hands. A player can make his or her hand signify a rock (clenched fist), a piece of paper (open palm) or a pair of scissors (first and second fingers outstretched). The winner is the person who overcomes the other, according to the following rules. A rock blunts scissors and therefore wins. Scissors cut paper and therefore win. Paper wraps a rock and therefore wins.

The dialogue between the computer and the player looks like this:

```
Hello
Choose r (for rock), s (for scissors), or p (for paper):
s
You chose scissors.
The computer chose paper
You won!

Another game?
n
Good Bye
```

```cpp
#include <iostream.h>
#include <stdlib.h>

int main (void)
{
    char reply;
    void play_game (void);

    cout << "Hello" << endl;
```

```
    reply='y';
    while (reply =='y')
        {
        play_game();
        cout << "Another game?" << endl;
        cin >> reply;
        }
    cout << "Good Bye";
}


void play_game (void)
{
    char human_choice, computer_choice;

    void Human_Go (char &);
    void Computer_Go(char &);
    void Decide_who_won (char, char);

    Human_Go (human_choice);
    Computer_Go (computer_choice);
    Decide_who_won (computer_choice, human_choice);
}


void Human_Go (char & choice)
{
    void display_choice (char);
    cout << "Choose r (for rock), s (for scissors), or p (for
      paper):"
        << endl;
    cin >> choice;
    cout << "You chose";
    display_choice (choice);
}


void display_choice (char choice)
{
    if (choice == 's') cout << "scissors";
    if (choice == 'r') cout << "rock";
    if (choice == 'p') cout << "paper";
    cout << endl;
}
```

```cpp
void Computer_Go (char & choice)
{
    int random_number;
    void display_choice (char);

    random_number=rand() % 3;

    if (random_number==0) choice='r';
    if (random_number==1) choice='s';
    if (random_number==2) choice='p';

    cout << "The computer chose";
    display_choice (choice);
}



void Decide_who_won (char computer, char human)
{
    if (computer==human)
        cout << "it's a draw!" << endl;
    else
        if ((computer=='p') && (human=='r')
            ||
            (computer=='r') && (human=='s')
            ||
            (computer=='s') && (human=='p'))
            cout << "Computer wins" << endl;
        else
            cout << "You win" << endl;
}
```

Index